MW01144416

Pocket San Francisco

Reprinted from *Fodor's San Francisco '94*

Fodor's Travel Publications, Inc.
New York • Toronto • London •
Sydney • Auckland

Fodor's Pocket San Francisco

Editors: Christopher Billy, Katherine Kane
Contributors: John Burks, Toni Chapman, Laura Del
Rosso, Pamela Faust, Sheila Gadsden, Jacqueline Kil-
leen, Daniel Mangin, Catherine McEver, Marcy
Pritchard, Linda K. Schmidt, Dan Spitzer, Robert
Taylor, Casey Tefertiller
Creative Director: Fabrizio La Rocca
Cartographer: David Lindroth
Illustrator: Karl Tanner
Cover Photograph: Stephenson/Westlight
Design: Vignelli Associates

Contents

Maps

Foreword

While every care has been taken to assure the accuracy of the information in this guide, the passage of time will always bring change and, consequently, the publisher cannot accept responsibility for errors that may occur.

All prices and opening times quoted here are based on information supplied to us at press time. Hours and admission fees may change, however, and the prudent traveler will avoid inconvenience by calling ahead.

Fodor's wants to hear about your travel experiences, both pleasant and unpleasant. When a hotel or restaurant fails to live up to its billing, let us know and we will investigate the complaint and revise our entries where the facts warrant it.

Send your letters to the editors of Fodor's Travel Publications, 201 E. 50th Street, New York, NY 10022.

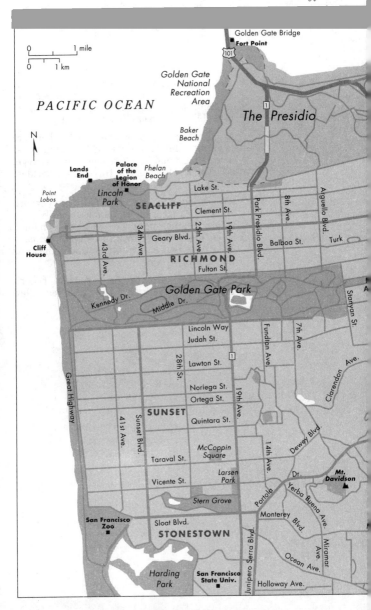

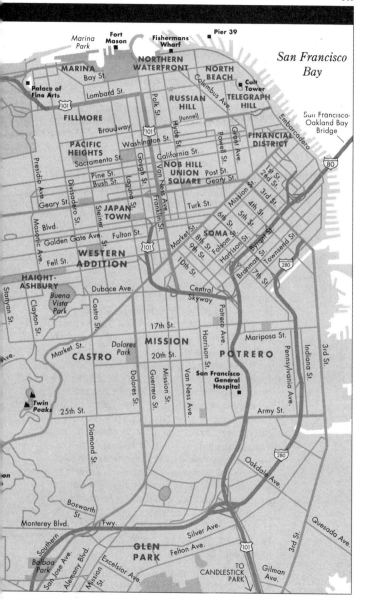

Marina Park
Fort Mason
Fishermans Wharf
Pier 39

San Francisco Bay

MARINA
Bay St.
NORTHERN WATERFRONT
NORTH BEACH
Columbus Ave.
Colt Tower
TELEGRAPH HILL

Palace of Fine Arts
Lombard St.
101
RUSSIAN HILL
(tunnel)

San Francisco-Oakland Bay Bridge

FILLMORE
Broadway
101
Hyde St.
Polk St.
Green Ave.
Powell St.
FINANCIAL DISTRICT
Embarcadero

PACIFIC HEIGHTS
Washington St.
California St.
NOB HILL
80

Presidio Ave.
Sacramento St.
Gough St.
Van Ness Ave.
Pine St.
Bush St.
UNION SQUARE
Post St.
Geary St.
1st St.
2nd St.
Mission St.
3rd St.
4th St.

Divisadero St.
Geary St.
Laguna St.
JAPAN-TOWN
Franklin St.
Turk St.
5th St.
6th St.

Masonic Ave.
Steiner St.
Golden Gate Ave.
Fulton St.
Market St.
7th St.
8th St.
SOMA
Folsom St.
Harrison St.
Bryant St.
Brannan St.
Townsend St.

WESTERN ADDITION
101
Fell St.
9th St.
10th St.

HAIGHT-ASHBURY
Stanyan St.
Buena Vista Park
Clayton St.
Dubace Ave.
Castro St.
Central Skyway
280
7th St.

Twin Peaks
Market St.
Dolores Park
17th St.
MISSION
20th St.
Harrison St.
Potrero Ave.
Mariposa St.
POTRERO
Pennsylvania Ave.
Indiana St.
3rd St.

CASTRO
25th St.
Dolores St.
Guerrero St.
Mission St.
Van Ness Ave.
San Francisco General Hospital
Army St.

Diamond St.
Oakdale Ave.
280

on

Bosworth St.
Fwy.
Quesada Ave.

Monterey Blvd.
Silver Ave.
Felton Ave.
101
3rd St.

Southern
Balboa Park
San Jose Ave.
Alemany Blvd.
Excelsior Ave.
Mission St.
GLEN PARK
TO CANDLESTICK PARK
Gilman Ave.

Introduction

San Franciscans tend to regard the envy of visitors as a matter of course and to look on whatever brought them to settle here (there's probably never been a time when the majority of the population was native born) as a brilliant stroke of luck. Certain local problems can be traced to this warm contentment with the city and to the attendant fear that somebody might do something to *change* it. The skyline, for example, which in recent decades has become clotted with high rises, has turned into a source of controversy. The city's Financial District is dominated by the dark, looming Bank of America—the sculpted lump of black granite out front has been nicknamed "The Banker's Heart"—and by the Transamerica Building, the glass-and-concrete pyramid that has made the city's skyline instantly recognizable. (Nearly two decades after its construction, San Franciscans still argue vehemently about its merits, or its utter lack of them. But nobody claims it isn't distinctive.) Admirers of the skyline defend the skyscrapers as evidence of prosperity and of San Francisco's world-class stature; detractors grumble about the "Manhattanization" that's ruining a unique place. Historically, San Francisco is a boomtown, and various periods of frantic building have lined the pockets of developers for whom the city's beauty was no consideration at all. Nevertheless, in 1986 the voters set limits on downtown construction; now the controversy has moved out to the neighborhoods, where entrepreneurs want to knock down single-family houses to make room for profitable apartment buildings.

The boom began in 1848. At the beginning of that year, San Francisco wasn't much more than a pleasant little settlement that had been founded by the Spaniards back in the auspicious year of 1776. The natural harbor of the bay (so commodious that "all the navies of the world might fit" inside it, as one visitor wrote) made it a village with a future. The future came abruptly when gold was discovered at John Sutter's sawmill in the Sierra foothills, some 115 miles to the northeast. By 1850, San Francisco's population had zoomed from 500 to 30,000, and a "western Wall Street" sprang up as millions upon millions of dollars' worth of gold was panned and blasted out of the hills. The gold mines began to dry up in a few years; but in 1859 prospectors turned up a fabulously rich vein of silver in the Virginia Range, in what is now Nevada; and San Francisco—the nearest financial center—prospered again.

Not so many centuries ago the area that was to become San Francisco was a windswept, virtually treeless, and, above all, sandy wasteland. Sand even covered the hills. The sand is still there, but—except along the ocean—it's well hidden. City Hall is built on 80 feet of it. The westerly section of the city—the Sunset and Richmond districts and Golden Gate Park—seems flat only because sand has filled in the contours of the hills.

But the hills that remain are spectacular. They provide vistas all over the city—nothing is more common than to find yourself staring out toward Angel Island or Alcatraz, or across the bay at Berkeley and Oakland. The hills are also exceptionally good at winding pedestrians. (The cable cars didn't become instantly popular because they were picturesque.) The city's two bridges, which are almost as majestic as their surroundings, had their 50th birthdays in 1986 and 1987. The Golden Gate Bridge, which crosses to Marin County, got a bigger party, but the San

Francisco-Oakland Bay Bridge got a better present: a necklace of lights along its spans. They were supposed to be temporary, but the locals were so taken with the glimmer that bridge boosters started a drive to make them permanent; radio DJs and newspaper columnists put out daily appeals, drivers gave extra quarters to the toll takers, various corporations put up shares, and—close to a million dollars later—the lights on the Bay Bridge now shine nightly.

The city has three trademarks: the fog, the cable cars, and the Victorians. Bay-windowed, ornately decorated Victorian houses—the multicolor, ahistorical paint jobs that have become popular make them seem even more ornate—are the city's most distinguishing architectural feature. They date mainly from the latter part of Queen Victoria's reign, 1870 to the turn of the century. In those three decades, San Francisco more than doubled in population (from 150,000 to 342,000); the transcontinental railway, linking the once-isolated western capital to the east, had been completed in 1869. That may explain the exuberant confidence of the architecture.

In terms of both geography and culture, San Francisco is about as close as you can get to Asia in the continental United States. (The city prides itself on its role as a Pacific Rim capital, and overseas investment has become a vital part of its financial life.) The first great wave of Chinese immigrants came during the gold rush in 1852. Chinese workers quickly became the target of race hatred and discriminatory laws; Chinatown—which began when the Chinese moved into old buildings that white businesses seeking more fashionable locations had abandoned—developed, as much as anything else, as a refuge. Chinatown is still a fascinating place to wander, and it's a good bet for late-night food, but it's not the whole story by any means. The Asian community, which now accounts for a fifth of San Francisco's population, reaches into every San Francisco neighborhood, and particularly into the Sunset and Richmond districts, out toward the ocean. Clement Street, which runs through the center of Richmond, has become the main thoroughfare of a second Chinatown. Southeast Asian immigrants, many of them ethnic Chinese, are transforming the seedy Tenderloin into a thriving Little Indochina. There was heavy Japanese immigration earlier in this century, but most of it went to southern California, where organized labor had less of a foothold and where there were greater opportunities for Asian workers. Still, San Francisco has its Japantown, with its massive Japan Center complex and scads of shops and restaurants clustered in and around it. In the past, Asians have tended toward a backseat—or at least an offstage—role in the city's politics; but like so much else on the city's cultural/political landscape, that, too, seems to be changing.

San Francisco has always been a loose, tolerant—some would say licentious—city. As early as the 1860s, the "Barbary Coast"—a collection of taverns, whorehouses, and gambling joints along Pacific Avenue close to the waterfront—was famous, or infamous. Bohemian communities seem to thrive here. In the 1950s, North Beach, the city's Little Italy, became the home of the Beat Movement. (Herb Caen, the city's best-known columnist, coined the term "beatnik.") Lawrence Ferlinghetti's City Lights, a bookstore and publishing house that brought out, among other titles, Allen Ginsberg's *Howl* and *Kaddish*, still stands on Columbus Avenue as a monument to the era. (Across Broadway, a plaque identifies the Condor as the site of the nation's first topless and bottomless performances, a monument to a slightly later era.) The Bay Area was the epicenter of '60s ferment, too. The Free Speech Movement began at the University of California in Berkeley (where, in October 1965, Allen Ginsberg introduced the term "flower power"), and Stanford's David Harris, who went to prison for defying the draft, numbered among the nation's most famous student leaders. In San Francisco, the Haight-Ashbury district was synonymous with hippiedom and gave rise to such legendary bands as the Jefferson Airplane, Big Brother and the Holding Company (fronted by Janis Joplin), and the Grateful Dead. Twenty years later, the Haight has become a peculiar mix. Haight Street itself is a shopping strip, replete with boutiques and nail-care salons and noted especially for its vintage-clothing stores. The once-funky Victorians that housed the communes have been restored and purchased by wealthy yuppies. The neighborhood's history and its name, however, still draw neo-hippies, as well as New Wavers with black lips and blue hair, and some rather menacing skinheads. The transients who sleep in nearby Golden Gate Park make panhandling one of the street's major business activities. It's not a completely happy mix; still, most of the residents remain committed to keeping the Haight the Haight. There's especially bitter resentment against the chain businesses (McDonald's, The Gap) that have moved in. In 1988 a chain drugstore's attempt to open a huge outlet sparked furious protest and, eventually, arson. The question of who set the fire, which gutted not only the unfinished store but several nearby apartments and businesses as well, has never been answered, but the fire accomplished its purpose: The chain pulled out.

Southwest of the Haight is the onetime Irish neighborhood known as the Castro, which during the 1970s became identified with lesbian and gay liberation. Castro Street is dominated by the elaborate Castro Theater, a 1923 vision in Spanish Baroque, which presents one of the best repertory movie schedules in the city. (The grand old pipe organ still plays during intermissions, breaking into "San Francisco" just before the feature begins.) There's been much talk, most of it exaggerated, about how AIDS has chastened and "matured" the Castro; it's still an effervescent neighborhood, and—as housing everywhere has become more and more of a prize—an increasingly mixed one. At the same time, gays, like Asians, are moving out of the ghetto and into neighborhoods all around the city.

The Lesbian and Gay Freedom Day Parade, each June, vies with the Chinese New Year Parade, in February, as the city's most elaborate. They both get competition from Japantown's Cherry Blossom Festival, in April; the Columbus Day and St. Patrick's Day parades; the June Carnaval in the Hispanic Mission District; and the May Day march, a labor celebration in a labor town. The mix of ethnic, economic, social, and sexual groups can be bewildering, but the city's residents—whatever their origin—face it with aplomb and even gratitude. Everybody in San Francisco has an opinion about where to get the best burrito or the hottest Szechuan eggplant or the strongest cappuccino. The most staid citizens have learned how to appreciate good camp. Nearly everyone smiles on the fortunate day they arrived on, or were born on, this windy, foggy patch of peninsula.

1 Essential Information

Before You Go

Visitor Information

Contact the **San Francisco Convention and Visitors Bureau** (201 3rd St., Suite 900, 94103, tel. 415/974–6900). The attractive 80-page *San Francisco Book* ($1; from the SFCVB at Box 6977, 94101) includes up-to-date information on theater offerings, art exhibits, sporting events, and other special happenings.

The **Redwood Empire Association Visitor Information Center** (785 Market St., 15th floor, 94103, 415/543–8334) covers San Francisco and surrounding areas, including the Wine Country, the redwood groves, and northwestern California. For a dollar postage they will also send *The Redwood Empire Visitor's Guide*.

In addition, there are chambers of commerce in dozens of San Francisco Bay Area towns, including **Berkeley** (1834 University Ave., Box 210, Berkeley, CA 94703, tel. 510/549–7003), and convention and visitors bureaus in **Oakland** (1000 Broadway, Suite 200, Oakland, CA 94607, tel. 510/839–9000 or 800/262–5526) and **San Jose** (333 W. San Carlos St., Suite 1000, San Jose, CA 95110, tel. 408/295–9600).

The **California Office of Tourism** (801 K St., Suite 1600, Sacramento, CA 95814, tel. 916/322–1397) can answer many questions about travel in the state. You can also order a detailed 208-page book, *Discover the Californias*, which includes an informative section on the Bay Area (free; tel. 800/862–2543).

Tips for British Travelers

Contact the **United States Travel and Tourism Administration** (Box 1 EN, London, W1A 1EN, tel. 071/495–4466).

Passports and Visas

British citizens need a valid 10-year passport.

A visa is not necessary unless (1) you are planning to stay more than 90 days; (2) your trip is for purposes other than vacation; (3) you have at some time been refused a visa, or refused admission, to the United States, or have been required to leave by the U.S. Immigration and Naturalization Service; or (4) you do not have a return or onward ticket. You will need to fill out the Visa Waiver Form, I-94W, supplied by the airline.

To apply for a visa or for more information, call the U.S. Embassy's Visa Information Line (tel. 0891/200–290; calls cost 48p per minute or 36p per minute cheap rate). If you qualify for the visa-free travel but want a visa anyway, you must apply in writing, enclosing a self-addressed envelope, to the U.S. Embassy's Visa Branch (5 Upper Grosvenor St., London W1A 2JB), or, for residents of Northern Ireland, to the U.S. Consulate General (Queen's House, Queen St., Belfast BT1 6EO). Submit a completed Nonimmigrant Visa Application (Form 156), a valid passport, a photograph, and evidence of your intended departure from the United States after a temporary visit. If you require a visa, call 0891/234–224 to schedule an interview.

Customs British visitors aged 21 or over may import the following into the United States: 200 cigarettes or 50 cigars or 2 kilograms of tobacco; one U.S. liter of alcohol; gifts to the value of $100. Restricted items include meat products, seeds, plants, and fruits. Never carry illegal drugs.

Returning to the United Kingdom you may import duty-free 200 cigarettes, 100 cigarillos, 50 cigars or 250 grams of tobacco; 1 liter of spirits or 2 liters of fortified or sparkling wine; 2 liters of still table wine; 60 milliliters of perfume; 250 milliliters of toilet water; plus £36 worth of other goods, including gifts and souvenirs.

For further information or a copy of "A Guide for Travelers," which details standard customs procedures as well as what you may bring into the United Kingdom from abroad, contact HM Customs and Excise (New King's Beam House, 22 Upper Ground, London SE1).

Insurance Most tour operators, travel agents, and insurance agents sell specialized policies covering accident, medical expenses, personal liability, trip cancellation, and loss or theft of personal property. Some policies include coverage for delayed departure and legal expenses, winter sports, accidents, or motoring abroad. You can also purchase an annual travel-insurance policy valid for every trip you make during the year in which it's purchased (usually only trips of less than 90 days). Before you leave, make sure you will be covered if you have a preexisting medical condition or are pregnant; your insurers may not pay for routine or continuing treatment, or may require a note from your doctor certifying your fitness to travel.

The **Association of British Insurers,** a trade association representing 450 insurance companies, advises extra medical coverage for visitors to the United States.

For advice by phone or a free booklet, "Holiday Insurance," that sets out what to expect from a holiday-insurance policy and gives price guidelines, contact the Association of British Insurers (51 Gresham St., London EC2V 7HQ, tel. 071/600–3333; 30 Gordon St., Glasgow G1 3PU, tel. 041/226–3905; Scottish Provincial Bldg., Donegall Sq. W, Belfast BT1 6JE, tel. 0232/249176; call for other locations).

Tour Operators Tour operators offering packages to San Francisco include **British Airways Holidays** (Atlantic House, Hazelwick Ave., Three Bridges, Crawley, West Sussex RH10 1NP, tel. 0293/611611), **Jetsave** (Sussex House, London Rd., East Grinstead, West Sussex RH19 1LD, tel. 0342/312033), **Key to America** (15 Feltham Rd., Ashford, Middlesex TW15 1DQ, tel. 0784/248777), **Kuoni Travel Ltd.** (Kuoni House, Dorking, Surrey RH5 4AZ, tel. 0306/76711), **Premier Holidays** (Premier Travel Center, Westbrook, Milton Rd., Cambridge CB4 1YQ, tel. 0223/355977), and **Trailfinders** (194 Kensington High St., London W8 7RG, tel. 071 937–5400; 58 Deansgate, Manchester, M3 2FF, tel. 061/839–6969).

Airfares Fares vary enormously. Fares from consolidators are usually the cheapest, followed by promotional fares such as APEX. A few phone calls should reveal the current picture. When comparing fares, don't forget to figure airport taxes and weekend supplements. Once you know which airline is going your way at the right time for the least money, book immediately, since seats at the lowest prices often sell out quickly. Travel agents will generally hold a reservation for up to five days, especially if you give a credit card number.

Some travel agencies that offer cheap fares to San Francisco include **Trailfinders** (42–50 Earl's Court Rd., London W8 6EJ, tel. 071/937–5400), specialists in Round-The-World fares and independent travel; **Travel Cuts** (295a Regent St., London W1R 7YA, tel. 071/637–3161), the Canadian Students' travel service; **Flightfile** (49 Tottenham Court Rd., London W1p 9RE, tel. 071/700–2722), a flight-only agency.

Car Rental Make the arrangements from home to avoid inconvenience, save money, and guarantee yourself a vehicle. Major firms include **Alamo** (tel. 0800/272–200), **Budget** (tel. 0800/181–181), **EuroDollar** (tel. 0895/233–300), **Europcar** (tel. 081/950–5050), and **Hertz** (tel. 081/679–1799).

In the United States you must be 21 to rent a car; rates may be higher for those under 25. Extra costs cover child seats, compulsory for children under 5 (about $3 per day); additional drivers (around $1.50 per day); and the all-but-compulsory Collision Damage Waiver. To pick up your reserved car, you will need the reservation voucher, a passport, a U.K. driver's license, and a travel insurance policy covering each driver.

Travelers with Main information sources include the **Royal As-**
Disabilities **sociation for Disability and Rehabilitation** (RADAR, 25 Mortimer St., London W1N 8AB, tel. 071/637–5400), which publishes travel information for the disabled in Britain and **Mobility International** (228 Borough High St., London SE1 1JX, tel. 071/403–5688), the headquarters of an international membership organization that serves as a clearinghouse of travel information for people with disabilities.

When to Go

Any time of the year is the right time to go to San Francisco, which is acknowledged to be one of the most beautiful cities in the world. The fog rolls in during the summer, but it seems less an inconvenience than part of the atmosphere.

San Francisco is on the tip of a peninsula, surrounded on three sides by the Pacific Ocean and San Francisco Bay. Its climate is quintessentially marine and moderate: It never gets very hot—anything above 80° is reported as a shocking heat wave—or very cold.

For all its moderation, however, San Francisco can be tricky. In the summertime, fog often rolls in from the ocean, blocking the sun and filling the air with dampness.

If you travel to the north, east, or south of the city, you will find warmer summer temperatures. Shirtsleeves and thin cottons are usually just fine for the Wine Country.

Be prepared for rain in winter, especially December and January. Winds off the ocean can add to the chill factor, so pack some warm clothing to be on the safe side.

Climate The following are average daily maximum and minimum temperatures for San Francisco.

Jan.	55F	13C	May	66F	19C	Sept.	73F	23C
	41	– 5		48	– 9		51	11
Feb.	59F	15C	June	69F	21C	Oct.	69F	21C
	42	– 6		51	11		50	10
Mar.	60F	16C	July	69F	21C	Nov.	64F	18C
	44	– 7		51	11		44	– 7
Apr.	62F	17C	Aug.	69F	21C	Dec.	57F	14C
	46	– 8		53	12		42	– 6

Information For current weather conditions for cities in the
Sources United States and abroad, plus the local time and helpful travel tips, call the **Weather Channel Connection** (tel. 900/WEATHER; 95¢ per minute) from a touch-tone phone.

What to Pack

Clothing The most important single rule to bear in mind when packing for a vacation in the San Francisco Bay Area is to prepare for changes in temperature. An hour's drive can take you up or down many degrees, and the variation from daytime to nighttime in a single location is often marked. Take along sweaters, jackets, and clothes for layering as your best insurance for coping with variations in temperature. Include shorts or cool cottons for summer. Always tuck in a bathing suit, because most lodgings include a pool.

Although casual dressing is a hallmark of the California lifestyle, men will need a jacket and tie for many good restaurants in the evening, and women will be more comfortable in something dressier than regulation sightseeing garb.

Bear in mind that San Francisco can be chilly at any time of the year, especially in summer, when the fog is apt to descend and stay. Nothing is more pitiful than the sight of uninformed tourists in shorts, their legs blue with cold. Take along clothes that will keep you warm, even if the season doesn't seem to warrant it.

Miscellaneous Although you can buy supplies of film, sunscreen lotion, aspirin, and most other necessities almost anywhere in California, it's a good idea to take along a reasonable supply of the things you know you will be using routinely, to spare yourself the bother of stocking up. An extra pair of glasses, contact lenses, or prescription sunglasses is always a good idea. Also pack any prescription medications you need regularly.

Luggage Regulations Free baggage allowances on an airline depend on the airline, the route, and the class of your ticket. In general, on domestic flights and on international flights between the United States and foreign destinations, you are entitled to check two bags—neither exceeding 62 inches, or 158 centimeters (length + width + height), or weighing more than 70 pounds (32 kilograms). A third piece may be brought aboard as a carryon; its total dimensions are generally limited to less than 45 inches (114 centimeters), so it will fit easily under the seat in front of you or in the overhead compartment. There are variations, so ask in advance. The only rule, a Federal Aviation Administration safety regulation that pertains to carry-on baggage on U.S. airlines, requires only that carryons be properly stowed and allows the airline to limit allowances and tailor them to different aircraft and operational conditions. Charges for excess, oversize, or overweight pieces vary, so inquire before you pack.

Arriving and Departing

By Plane

Flights are either nonstop, direct, or connecting. A **nonstop** flight requires no change of plane and makes no stops. A **direct** flight stops at least once and can involve a change of plane, although the flight number remains the same; if the first leg is late, the second waits. This is not the case with a **connecting** flight, which involves a different plane and a different flight number.

San Francisco International Airport is just south of the city, off U.S. 101. American carriers serving San Francisco are **Alaska Air, American, Continental, Delta, Southwest, TWA, United,** and **USAir.** International carriers include **Air New Zealand, British Airways, Canadian Airlines, Canadian Pacific, China Airlines, Japan Air Lines, Lufthansa, Mexicana,** and **Qantas.** Several domestic airlines serve the Oakland Airport, which is across the bay but not much farther away from downtown San Francisco (via I–880 and I–80), although traffic on the Bay Bridge may at times make travel time longer.

Enjoying the Flight Because the air aloft is dry, drink plenty of beverages while on board; remember that drinking alcohol contributes to jet lag, as do heavy meals. Sleepers usually prefer window seats to curl up against; restless passengers ask to be on the aisle. Bulkhead seats, in the front row of each cabin, have more legroom, but since there's no seat ahead, trays attach awkwardly to the arms of your seat, and you must stow all possessions overhead. Bulkhead seats are usually reserved for the disabled, the elderly, and people traveling with babies.

Smoking Since February 1990, smoking has been banned on all domestic flights of less than six hours' duration; the ban also applies to domestic segments of international flights aboard U.S. and foreign carriers.

Between the Airport and Downtown **SFO Airporter** (tel. 415/495–8404) provides bus service between downtown and the airport, making the round of downtown hotels. Buses run every 20 minutes from 5 AM to 11 PM, from the lower level outside the baggage claim area. The fare is $7 one-way, $11 round-trip.

For $11, **Supershuttle** will take you from the airport to anywhere within the city limits of San Francisco. At the airport, after picking up your luggage, call 415/871–7800 and a van will pick you up within five minutes. To go to the airport, make reservations (tel. 415/558–8500) 24 hours in advance. The Supershuttle stops at the upper level of the terminal, along with several other bus and van transport services.

Taxis to or from downtown take 20–30 minutes and average $30.

By Train

Amtrak (tel. 800/872–7245) trains (the *Zephyr*, from Chicago via Denver, and the *Coast Starlight*, traveling between San Diego and Seattle) stop in Oakland; from there buses will take you across the Bay Bridge to the Transbay Terminal at 1st and Mission streets in San Francisco.

By Bus

Greyhound serves San Francisco from the Transbay Terminal at 1st and Mission streets (tel. 415/558–6789).

By Car

Route I–80 finishes its westward journey from New York's George Washington Bridge at the Bay Bridge, linking Oakland and San Francisco. U.S. 101, running north–south through the entire state, enters the city across the Golden Gate Bridge and continues south down the peninsula, along the west side of the bay.

Staying in San Francisco

Important Addresses and Numbers

Tourist Information The **San Francisco Convention and Visitors Bureau** (tel. 415/974–6900 or 415/391–2001 for a summary of daily events) maintains a visitor information center on the lower level at Hallidie Plaza (Powell and Market streets), just three blocks from Union Square, near the cable car turnaround and the Powell Street entrance to BART. It's open weekdays 9–5, Saturdays 9–3, and Sundays 10–2.

The **Redwood Empire Association Visitor Information Center** on the 15th floor at 785 Market Street (tel. 415/543–8334) is open weekdays 9 AM–4:30 AM.

Emergencies   For **police** or **ambulance,** telephone 911.

Doctors   Two hospitals with 24-hour emergency rooms are **San Francisco General Hospital** (1001 Potrero Ave., tel. 415/206–8000) and the **Medical Center at the University of California, San Francisco** (500 Parnassus Ave. at 3rd Ave., near Golden Gate Park, tel. 415/476–1000).

Access Health Care provides drop-in medical care at two San Francisco locations, daily 8–8. No membership is necessary. *Davies Medical Center, Castro St. at Duboce Ave., tel. 415/565–6600; 26 California St. at Drumm St., tel. 415/397–2881.*

Pharmacies   Several **Walgreen Drug Stores** have 24-hour pharmacies, including stores at 500 Geary Street near Union Square (tel. 415/673–8413) and 3201 Divisadero Street at Lombard Street (tel. 415/931–6417). Also try the Walgreen pharmacy at 135 Powell Street near Market Street (tel. 415/391–7222), which is open Monday–Saturday 8 AM–midnight, Sunday 9 AM–8 PM.

Getting Around San Francisco

Because San Francisco is relatively compact and because it's so difficult to find parking, we recommend that you do your exploring on foot or by bus as much as possible. You may not need a car at all, except perhaps for exploring the Presidio, Golden Gate Park, Lincoln Park, the Western Shoreline, and for making excursions out of town.

How to Get There from Union Square will tell you how to reach approximately 50 points of interest in the city by public transportation. It's free from the Redwood Empire Association Visitor Information Center (*see* Tourist Information in Important Addresses and Numbers, *above*).

By BART **Bay Area Rapid Transit** (tel. 415/788–2278) sends air-conditioned aluminum trains at speeds of up to 80 miles an hour across the bay to Oakland, Berkeley, Concord, Richmond, and Fremont. Trains also travel south from San Francisco as far as Daly City. Wall maps in the stations list destinations and fares (85¢–$3). Trains run Monday–Saturday 6 AM–midnight, Sunday 9 AM–midnight.

A $2.60 excursion ticket buys a three-county tour. You can visit any of the 34 stations for up to four hours as long as you exit and enter at the same station.

By Bus The **San Francisco Municipal Railway System,** or **Muni** (tel. 415/673–6864), includes buses and trolleys, surface streetcars, and the new below-surface streetcars, as well as cable cars. There is 24-hour service, and the fare is $1 for adults, 35¢ for senior citizens and children 5–17. Exact change is always required; Muni does not offer free transfers.

A $6 pass good for unlimited travel all day on all routes can be purchased from ticket machines at cable car terminals and at the Visitor Information Center in Hallidie Plaza (Powell and Market Sts.).

By Cable Car In June 1984, the 109-year-old system returned to service after a $58.2 million overhaul. Because the cable cars had been declared a National Historic Landmark in 1964, renovation methods and materials had to preserve the historical and traditional qualities of Andrew Hallidie's system. The rehabilitated moving landmark has been designed to withstand another century of use.

The Powell-Mason line (No. 59) and the Powell-Hyde line (No. 60) begin at Powell and Market streets near Union Square and terminate at Fisherman's Wharf. The California Street line (No. 61) runs east and west from Market Street near the Embarcadero to Van Ness Avenue.

Cable cars are popular, crowded, and an experience to ride: Move toward one quickly as it pauses, wedge yourself into any available space, and hold on! The sensation of moving up and down some of San Francisco's steepest hills in a small, open-air clanging conveyance is not to be missed.

The fare (for one direction) is $2 for adults, $1 for children 5–17. Exact change is required. There are self-service ticket machines (which do make change) at terminals and major stops; be wary of street people attempting to "help" you buy a ticket.

By Taxi Rates are high in the city, although most rides are relatively short. It is almost impossible to hail a passing cab, especially on weekends. Either phone or use the nearest hotel taxi stand to grab a cab. See the Yellow Pages for numbers of taxi companies.

By Car Driving in San Francisco can be a challenge because of the hills, the one-way streets, and the traffic. Take it easy, remember to curb your wheels when parking on hills, and use public transportation whenever possible. On certain streets, parking is forbidden during rush hours. Look for the warning signs; illegally parked cars are towed. Downtown parking lots are often full and always expensive. Finding a spot in North Beach at night, for instance, may be impossible.

Guided Tours

In selecting a tour, bear in mind that the size of the vehicle will affect the character of the tour to some degree. Smaller vans can go to spots where the larger buses cannot maneuver or are not permitted, such as the Marina and the Palace of Fine Arts. Drivers of vans are sometimes more amenable to stopping for picture taking.

Unless specifically noted, the costs given for guided tours do not include meals or refreshments.

Orientation Tours **Golden City Tours** offers 14-passenger vans for their five-hour city tours, which include such landmarks as Twin Peaks, the Cliff House, and Chinatown as well as a drive across the Golden Gate Bridge. Customers are picked up at all major airport hotels. A shorter afternoon tour omits Sausalito. *Tel. 415/692–3044. Tours daily.*

Make reservations the day before. Cost: $28. Afternoon tour $18.50.

Golden Gate Tours uses both vans and buses for its 3½-hour city tour, offered mornings and afternoons. You can combine the tour with a bay cruise. Customers are picked up at hotels and motels. Senior-citizen and group rates are available. *Tel. 415/788–5775. Tours daily. Make reservations the day before. Cost: $22.50 adults, $11 children under 12, $20.50 senior citizens. Cruise combo: $30 adults, $15 children under 12, $28 senior citizens.*

Gray Line offers a variety of tours of the city, the Bay Area, and northern California. The city tour, on buses or double-decker buses, lasts 3½ hours and departs from the Transbay Terminal at 1st and Mission streets five to six times daily. Gray Line also picks up at centrally located hotels. **Gray Line-Cable Car Tours** sends motorized cable cars on a one-hour loop from Union Square to Fisherman's Wharf and two-hour tours including the Presidio, Japantown, and the Golden Gate Bridge. *Tel. 415/558–9400. Tours daily. Make reservations the day before. Cost: $23.50 adults, $11.75 children. Cable car tours, $12 and $18 adults, $6 and $9 children. No reservations necessary.*

The Great Pacific Tour uses 13-passenger vans for its daily 3½-hour city tour. Bilingual guides may be requested. They pick up at major San Francisco hotels. Tours are available to Monterey, the Wine Country, and Muir Woods. *Tel. 415/626–4499. Tours daily. Make reservations the day before, or, possibly, the same day. Cost: $25 adults, $24 senior citizens, $20 children 5–11.*

Superior Sightseeing Company operates 20-passenger vans and picks up visitors at hotels for 3½-hour tours of the city, ending at Fisherman's Wharf. There is also a full-day excursion to Wine Country. *Tel. 415/550–1352. Cost: $24–$40 adults, $22–$38 senior citizens, $12–$20 children.*

2 Exploring San Francisco

By Toni
Chapman

Updated by
Daniel
Mangin

"You could live in San Francisco a month and ask no greater entertainment than walking through it," waxed Inez Hayes Irwin, the author of *The Californiacs*, an effusive 1921 homage to the state of California and the City by the Bay. Her claim remains as true as ever today, and, as in the '20s, touring on foot is the best way to experience this diverse metropolis.

San Francisco is a relatively small city, with fewer than 750,000 residents nested on a 46.6-square-mile tip of land between San Francisco Bay and the Pacific Ocean. San Franciscans cherish the city's colorful past, and many older buildings have been spared from demolition and nostalgically converted into modern offices and shops. Longtime locals rue the sites that got away—spectacular railroad- and mining-boom-era residences lost in the '06 quake, the elegant Fox Theater, Playland at the Beach. But despite acts of God, the indifference of developers, and the at best mixed record of the city's Planning Commission, much of architectural and historical interest remains. Bernard Maybeck, Julia Morgan, Willis Polk, and Arthur Brown, Jr., are among the noted architects whose designs still grace the city's downtown and neighborhoods.

San Francisco's charms are both great and small. First-time visitors won't want to miss Golden Gate Park, the Palace of Fine Arts, the Golden Gate Bridge, or an exhilarating cable-car ride. A walk down the Filbert Steps or through Macondray Lane, though, or a peaceful hour gazing east from Ina Coolbrith Park, can be equally inspiring.

It's no accident that the San Francisco Bay Area has been a center for the environmental movement. An awareness of geographical setting permeates San Francisco life, with ever-present views of the surrounding mountains, ocean, and bay. Much of the city's neighborhood vitality comes from the distinct borders provided by its hills and valleys, and many areas are so named: Nob Hill, Twin Peaks, Eureka Valley, the East Bay. San Francisco neighborhoods are self-aware, and they retain strong cultural, political, and ethnic identities. Locals know this pluralism is the real life of the city. If you want to experience San Francisco, don't just stay downtown, visit the neighborhoods: the bustling Mission District, gay Castro, freaky Haight Street, serene Pacific Heights, historic Chinatown, still-exotic North Beach.

To do so you must navigate a maze of one-way streets and restricted parking zones. Public parking garages or lots tend to be expensive, as are the hotel parking spaces. The famed 40-plus hills can be a problem for drivers who are new to the terrain. Those museums on wheels—the cable cars—or the numerous buses or trolleys can take you to or near many of the area's attractions. In the exploring tours that follow, we have often included information on public transportation.

Highlights for First-Time Visitors

Chinatown (*see* Tour 6)
Cliff House (*see* Tour 17)
Coit Tower (*see* Tour 7)
Cruise to Alcatraz Island (*see* Tour 14)
Golden Gate Bridge (*see* Tour 15)
Japanese Tea Garden (*see* Tour 16)
Pacific Heights (*see* Tour 11)
Union Square (*see* Tour 1)

Tour 1: Union Square

Numbers in the margin correspond to points of interest on the Downtown San Francisco: Tours 1–13 map.

Since 1850 Union Square has been the heart of San Francisco's downtown. Its name derives from a series of violent pro-Union demonstrations staged in this hilly area just prior to the Civil War. This area is where you will find the city's finest department stores and its most elegant boutiques. There are 40 hotels within a three-block walk of the square, and the downtown theater district is nearby.

The square itself is a 2.6-acre oasis planted with palms, boxwood, and seasonal flowers, peopled with a kaleidoscope of characters: office workers sunning and brown-bagging, street musicians, always at least one mime, several vocal and determined preachers, and the ever-increasing parade of panhandlers. Throughout the year, the square hosts numerous public events: fashion shows, free noontime concerts, ethnic celebrations, and noisy demonstrations.

❶ Any visitor's first stop should be the **San Francisco Visitors Information Center** (tel. 415/391–2000) on the lower level of Hallidie Plaza at Powell and Market streets. It is open daily, and the multilingual staff will answer specific questions as well as provide maps, brochures, and information on daily events. The office provides 24-hour recorded information (tel. 415/391–2001).

❷ The **cable-car terminus** at Powell and Market streets is the starting point for two of the three operating lines. The Powell-Mason line climbs up Nob Hill, then winds through North Beach to Fisherman's Wharf. The Powell-Hyde car also crosses Nob Hill, but then continues up Russian Hill and down Hyde Street to Victorian Park across from the Buena Vista Cafe and near Ghirardelli Square.

Andrew Hallidie introduced the system in 1873 when he demonstrated his first car on Clay Street. In 1964 the tramlike vehicles were designated national historic landmarks. Before 1900 there were 600 cable cars spanning a network of 100 miles. Today there are 39 cars in the three lines, and the network covers just 12 miles. Most of the cars date from the last century, although the cars and lines had a complete $58 million overhaul during the early 1980s. There are seats for about 30 passengers, with usually that number standing or strap-hanging. If possible, plan your cable car ride for mid-morning or mid-afternoon during the week to avoid crowds. In summertime there are often long lines to board any of the three systems. Buy your ticket ($2, good in one direction) at nearby hotels or at the police/information booths near the turnaround. (*See* Getting Around by Cable Car in Chapter 1, Essential Information.)

Two helpful tips: The array of panhandlers, street preachers, and other regulars at this terminus can be daunting. Since you're going to stand in line anyway, you might want to do so at the Hyde Street end of the Powell-Hyde line,

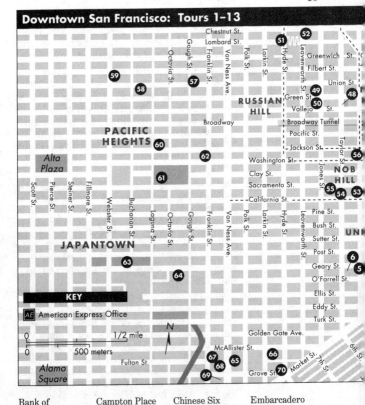

Downtown San Francisco: Tours 1–13

Chestnut St.
Lombard St.
Greenwich St.
Filbert St.
Union St.

RUSSIAN HILL
Green St.
Vallejo St.
Broadway Tunnel
Pacific St.
Jackson St.

PACIFIC HEIGHTS

Washington St.
Clay St.
Sacramento St.
California St.

NOB HILL

Pine St.
Bush St.
Sutter St.
Post St.
Geary St.
O'Farrell St.
Ellis St.
Eddy St.
Turk St.

JAPANTOWN

Golden Gate Ave.
McAllister St.
Grove St.

Broadway

Alta Plaza

Alamo Square

Fulton St.

Chestnut St. · Lombard St. · Gough St. · Franklin St. · Van Ness Ave. · Polk St. · Larkin St. · Hyde St. · Leavenworth St. · Taylor St. · Jones St.

Octavia St. · Scott St. · Pierce St. · Steiner St. · Fillmore St. · Webster St. · Buchanan St. · Laguna St. · Octavia St. · Gough St. · Franklin St. · Van Ness Ave. · Polk St. · Larkin St. · Hyde St. · Leavenworth St.

Market St. · 6th St. · 7th St.

KEY

AE American Express Office

0 ——— 1/2 mile
0 ——— 500 meters

N

Bank of America, **17**	Campton Place Hotel, **9**	Chinese Six Companies, **40**	Embarcadero Center, **25**
Buddha's Universal Church, **38**	Center for the Arts, **29**	City Hall, **65**	Ferry Building, **22**
Cable Car Museum, **56**	Chinatown Gate, **31**	City Lights Bookstore, **45**	Feusier House, **49**
Cable-car terminus, **2**	Chinese Cultural Center, **35**	Coit Tower, **47**	450 Sutter Street, **13**
	Chinese Hist. Society, **36**	Crocker Galleria, **12**	Geary, **5**
		Curran, **6**	Grace Cathedral, **54**

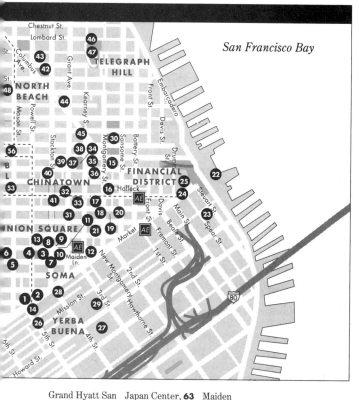

legend continues

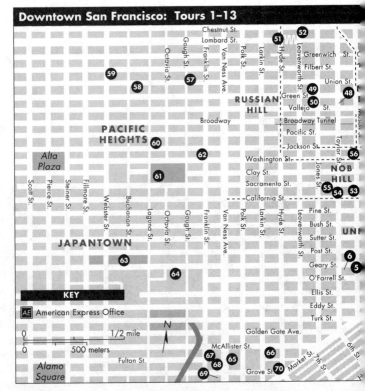

Downtown San Francisco: Tours 1–13

San Francisco Bay

which affords views of the bay and Golden Gate Bridge while you wait. Not to mention less racket. (*See* Tour 14: The Northern Waterfront, *below.*) Better yet, if it's just the experience of riding a cable car you're after (rather than a trip to the wharf or Nob Hill), try boarding the less-busy California line at Van Ness Avenue and ride it down to the Hyatt Regency. (*See* Tour 11: Pacific Heights, *below.*)

❸ A two-block stroll north along bustling Powell Street leads to **Union Square** itself. At center stage, the Victory Monument by Robert Ingersoll Aitken commemorates Commodore George Dewey's victory over the Spanish fleet at Manila in 1898. The 97-foot Corinthian column, topped by a bronze figure symbolizing naval conquest, was dedicated by Theodore Roosevelt in 1903 and withstood the 1906 earthquake.

After the earthquake and fire in 1906, the square was dubbed "Little St. Francis" because of the temporary shelter erected for residents of the St. Francis Hotel. Actor John Barrymore was among the guests pressed into volunteering to stack bricks in the square. His uncle, thespian John Drew, remarked, "It took an act of God to get John out of bed and the United States government to get him to work."

❹ The **Westin St. Francis Hotel,** on the southwest corner of Post and Powell, was built here in 1904 and was gutted by the 1906 disaster. The second-oldest hotel in the city was conceived by Charles Crocker and his associates as an elegant hostelry for their millionaire friends. Swift service and sumptuous surroundings were hallmarks of the property. A sybarite's dream, the hotel's Turkish baths had ocean water piped in. A new, larger, more luxurious residence was opened in 1907 to attract loyal clients from among the world's rich and powerful. The hotel has known its share of notoriety as well; in 1975, Sara Jane Moore tried to shoot then-president Gerald R. Ford in front of the building. The ever-helpful staff will, however, gladly direct you to the traditional teatime ritual—or, if you prefer, to champagne and caviar—in the dramatic Art Deco Compass Rose lounge. Elaborate Chinese screens, secluded seating alcoves, and soothing background music make it an ideal time-out after frantic shopping or sightseeing. A ride up the glass elevators yields striking views of Union Square and beyond. On the 30th floor is Victor's, a cozy, book-lined restaurant, convenient for dining before or after the theater.

5 Both the Geary and Curran theaters are a few blocks west on Geary Street. The **Geary** (415 Geary St., tel. 415/749–2228), built in 1910, is home of the American Conservatory Theatre. Now in its 27th season, A.C.T. is one of North America's leading repertory companies. The 1,300-seat house normally offers a 34-week season to 20,000 subscribers, presenting both classical and contemporary dramas. The theater was closed indefinitely as a result of the October 1989 earthquake, and currently productions are being run at the Stage Door theater (420 Mason St.) and elsewhere until repairs are complete, possibly in time for the 1994–95 season. Its main **6** box office remains open. The **Curran** (445 Geary St., tel. 415/474–3800) is noted for showcasing traveling companies of Broadway shows. Farther up the street, and a must for film buffs, is the **Cinema Shop** (604 Geary St., tel. 415/885–6785), a tiny storefront jammed with posters, stills, lobby cards and rare videotapes of Hollywood classics and schlock films alike.

7 **TIX Bay Area,** formerly known as STBS, has a booth on the Stockton Street side of Union Square, opposite Maiden Lane. It provides day-of-performance tickets (cash or traveler's checks only) to all types of performing arts events at half-price, as well as regular full-price box-office services. Telephone reservations are not accepted for half-price tickets. You can also buy $10 Golden Gate Park Cultural Passes here, which get you into all of the park's museums at a bargain rate. *Tel. 415/433–7827. Open Tues.– Thurs. 11–6, Fri. and Sat. 11–7.*

8 Just a dash up from TIX Bay Area, the **Grand Hyatt San Francisco** (345 Stockton St.) offers exciting city views from its lounge, the Club 36. Stop and examine sculptor Ruth Asawa's fantasy fountain honoring the city's hills, bridges, and unusual architecture plus a wonder world of real and mythical creatures. Children and friends helped the artist shape the hundreds of tiny figures from baker's clay; these were assembled on 41 large panels from which molds were made for the bronze casting. Asawa's distinctive designs decorate many public areas in the city. You can see her famous mermaid fountain at Ghirardelli Square.

9 Across the street is the small, deluxe **Campton Place Hotel** (340 Stockton St., tel. 415/955–5555). Opened in 1983, it is the ultimate in quiet elegance and superior service. During the week the dining room is crowded with the city's movers and shakers; on Sunday morning, however, a more mellow group of locals and out-of-towners come to enjoy what may be the best brunch in San Francisco.

10 Pop around the corner into **Maiden Lane,** which runs from Stockton to Kearny streets. Known as Morton Street in the raffish Barbary Coast era, this red-light district reported at least one murder a week. But the 1906 fire destroyed the brothels and the street emerged as Maiden Lane. It has since become a chic and costly mall. The two blocks are closed to vehicles from 11 AM until 4 PM. During the day, take-out snacks can be enjoyed while resting under the gay, umbrella-shaded tables. Masses of daffodils and bright blossoms and balloons bedeck the lane during the annual spring festival. A carnival mood prevails, with zany street musicians, artsy-craftsy people, and throngs of spectators.

11 Note **140 Maiden Lane:** This handsome brick structure is the only Frank Lloyd Wright building in San Francisco. With its circular interior ramp and skylights, it is said to have been a model for his designs for the Guggenheim Museum in New York. It now houses the Circle Gallery, a showcase of contemporary artists. Be sure to study the unique limited-edition art jewelry designed by internationally acclaimed Erté. *Open Mon.–Sat. 10–6, Sun. noon–5.*

12 The **Crocker Galleria** (Post and Kearny Sts., tel. 415/392–0100) is an imaginatively designed three-level complex of fine dining and shopping establishments capped by a dazzling glass dome. One block north of Post, Sutter Street is lined by prestigious art galleries, antiques dealers, smart hotels, and noted designer boutiques. Art Deco aficionados will want to linger at the striking medical/dental office building at **450 Sutter Street.** Handsome Mayan-inspired designs are used in both exterior and interior surfaces of the 1930 terra-cotta-colored skyscraper.

Time Out Most stores and shops here open at about 9:30–10 AM. Venturing out early and settling down to a leisurely breakfast before the day's traffic and shoppers hit in full force is a nice way to ease into a busy day of sightseeing. **Mama's** (398 Geary St.) has always been a favorite for either light or full-breakfast selections.

Many of San Francisco's leading fine-arts galleries are around Union Square. Among them are **John Berggruen** (one of several establishments at 228 Grant Ave., tel. 415/781–4629; open weekdays 9:30–5:30, Sat. 10:30–5) and **Erika Meyerovich** (231 Grant Ave., tel. 415/421–9997; open weekdays 9–6, Sat. 10–5:30). At 49 Geary Street are **Fraenkel** (tel. 415/981–2661; open Tues.–Fri. 10:30–5:30, Sat. 11–5) and **Robert Koch** (tel. 415/421–0122; open Tues.–Sat. 11–5:30), both of which showcase contemporary and historic photographs.

Across Market Street from the cable car turnaround, the rehabilitated corner of 5th Street is now occupied by the gleaming **San Francisco Shopping Centre.** Opened in 1988, this urban mall is anchored by the huge **Nordstrom's** department store. Its glass-topped circular court and spiral escalators lead to more than 35 other stores. A big hit since the day it opened in 1992 is the two-floor **Warner Bros.** shop, which carries T-shirts, posters, books, and other mementos of the studio's past and present. Foot-weary shoppers can rejuvenate themselves at **Spa** on the fifth floor, or lunch in the **City Centre Grille,** overlooking Market Street.

Tour 2: The Financial District

The heart of San Francisco's financial district is Montgomery Street. It was here in 1848 that Sam Brannan proclaimed the historic gold dis-

covery on the American River. At that time, all
the streets below Montgomery between California and Broadway were wharves. At least 100
ships were abandoned by frantic crews and passengers all caught up in the '49 gold fever. Many
of the wrecks served as warehouses or were
used as foundations for new constructions.

The financial district is roughly bordered by
Kearny Street on the west, Washington Street
on the north, and Market Street on the southeast. On workdays it is a congested canyon of
soaring skyscrapers, gridlock traffic, and bustling pedestrians. In the evenings and on weekends the quiet streets allow walkers to admire
the distinctive architecture. Unfortunately, the
museums in corporate headquarters are closed
then.

The city's most photographed high rise is the
15 853-foot **Transamerica Pyramid** at 600 Montgomery Street, between Clay and Washington
streets at the end of Columbus Avenue. Designed by William Pereira and Associates in
1972, the controversial $34 million symbol has
become more acceptable to local purists over
time. There is a public viewing area on the 27th
floor (open weekdays 8–4). You can relax in a
redwood grove along the east side of the building.

A block-and-a-half down Montgomery Street is
16 the **Wells Fargo Bank History Museum.** There
were no formal banks in San Francisco during
the early years of the gold rush, and miners often entrusted their gold dust to saloon keepers.
In 1852, Wells Fargo opened its first bank in the
city, and the company established banking offices in the Mother Lode camps using stage-
coaches and pony express riders to service the
burgeoning state. (California's population
boomed from 15,000 to 200,000 between 1848
and 1852.) The History Museum displays sam-
ples of nuggets and gold dust from major mines,
a mural-size map of the Mother Lode, original
art by Western artists Charlie Russell and
Maynard Dixon, mementos of the poet bandit
Black Bart, and letters of credit and old bank
drafts. The showpiece is the red, century-old
Concord stagecoach that in the mid-1850s car-

ried 15 passengers from St. Louis to San Francisco in three weeks. *420 Montgomery St. Admission free. Open banking days 9–5.*

❶⑦ The granite-and-marble **Bank of America** building dominates the territory bounded by California, Pine, Montgomery, and Kearny streets. The 52-story polished red granite complex is crowned by a chic cocktail and dining restaurant. As in almost all corporate headquarters, the interiors display impressive original art, while outdoor plazas include avant-garde sculptures. In the mall a massive abstract black granite sculpture designed by the Japanese artist Masayuki has been dubbed the "Banker's Heart" by local wags.

Soaring 52 stories above the financial district, the Bank of America's **Carnelian Room** (tel. 415/433–7500) offers elegant and pricey dining with a nighttime view of the city lights. This is an excellent spot for a drink at sunset. By day, the room is the exclusive Banker's Club, open to members or by invitation. For a Chinese dinner with a French touch, try **Tommy Toy's** (655 Montgomery St.). Toy has re-created the opulent splendor of the 19th-century Empress Dowager's reading room. (The prices reflect the decor.)

⑱ The **Russ Building** (235 Montgomery St.) was called "the skyscraper" when it was built in 1927. The Gothic design was modeled after the Chicago Tribune Tower, and until the 1960s was San Francisco's tallest—at just 31 stories. Prior to the 1906 earthquake and fire, the site was occupied by the Russ House, considered one of the finest hostelries in the city.

⑲ The **Mills Building and Tower** (220 Montgomery St.) was the outstanding prefire building in the financial district. The 10-story all-steel construction had its own electric plant in the basement. The original Burnham and Root design of white marble and brick was erected in 1891–92. Damage from the 1906 fire was slight; its walls were somewhat scorched but were easily refurbished. Two compatible additions east on Bush Street were added in 1914 and 1918 by Willis Polk, and in 1931 a 22-story tower completed the design.

Ralph Stackpole's monumental 1930 granite sculptural groups, *Earth's Fruitfulness* and *Man's Inventive Genius,* flank another impos-
(20) ing structure, the **Pacific Stock Exchange** (which dates from 1915), on the south side of Pine Street at Sansome Street. The Stock Exchange Tower around the corner at 155 Sansome Street, a 1930 modern classic by architects Miller and Pfleuger, features an Art Deco gold ceiling and black marble-walled entry. *301 Pine St., 94104, tel. 415/393–4000. Tours by 2-week advance reservation; minimum 8 persons.*

Stroll down Sansome Street and turn right on
(21) Sutter Street. The **Hallidie Building** (130 Sutter St. between Kearny and Montgomery Sts.) was built as an investment by the University of California Regents in 1918 and named for cable car inventor and university regent Andrew S. Hallidie. Best viewed from across the street, it is believed to be the world's first all-glass-curtain-wall structure. Architect Willis Polk's revolutionary design hangs a foot beyond the reinforced concrete of the frame. It dominates the block with its reflecting glass, decorative exterior fire escapes that appear to be metal balconies, the Venetian Gothic cornice, and horizontal ornamental bands of birds at feeders.

Time Out   At lunchtime on weekdays you can rub elbows with power brokers and politicians in venerable **Jack's Restaurant** (615 Sacramento St., tel. 415/ 986–9854). Opened in 1864 and a survivor of the quake, Jack's is a purveyor of traditional American fare—steaks, chops, seafood, and stews. Reservations are suggested. For excellent fresh seafood, San Franciscans in the know go to **Sam's Grill** (374 Bush St., tel. 415/421–0594). It's so popular for lunch you must arrive before 11:30 for even a chance at a table. Dinner service stops at 8:30, and Sam's is closed on weekends.

Heading back toward the Union Square retail area, don't miss the colorful **Hammersmith Building** at 301 Sutter Street. The small Beaux-Arts building structure was completed in 1907. Here again the extensive use of glass is noteworthy, as is the highly playful design.

Tour 3: The Embarcadero and Lower Market Street

In one instance, the 1989 Loma Prieta earthquake changed San Francisco for the better: The Embarcadero freeway had to be torn down, making the foot of Market Street clearly visible for the first time in 30 years. The trademark of **②** the port is the quaint **Ferry Building** that stands at the Embarcadero. The clock tower is 230 feet high and was modeled by Arthur Page Brown after the campanile of Seville's cathedral. The four great clock faces on the tower, powered by the swinging action of a 14-foot pendulum, stopped at 5:17 on the morning of April 18, 1906, and stayed that way for the following 12 months. The 1896 building survived the quake and is now the headquarters of the Port Commission and the World Trade Center. A waterfront promenade that extends from this point to the San Francisco—Oakland Bay Bridge is great for jogging, watching the sailboats on the bay (if the day is not too windy), or enjoying a picnic. Check out the beautiful new pedestrian pier adjacent to Pier 1, with its old-fashioned lamps, wrought-iron benches, and awe-inspiring views of the bay. Ferries from behind the Ferry Building sail to Sausalito, Larkspur, and Tiburon.

Walking south of the Ferry Building, you won't be able to miss the five-foot-wide, 2½-mile-long glass-and-concrete Promenade Ribbon. Billed by the city as the "longest art form in the nation," upon its completion in 1995 the artwork will span the waterfront from the base of Telegraph Hill to China Basin.

As you continue down the promenade, notice the curiously styled Audiffred Building at the corner of Mission Street and the Embarcadero. It was built by a homesick gentleman who wanted a reminder of his native France. Cross the Embarcadero at Howard Street, and turn right on Steuart Street.

Across Steuart Street from the main entrance **㉓** to the hotel is the new—and old—**Rincon Center.** Two modern office/apartment towers overlook a small shopping and restaurant mall behind an old post office built in the Streamline

Moderne Style. A stunning five-story rain column draws immediate attention in the mall. In the "Historic Lobby" (which formerly housed the post office's walk-up windows) is a mural by Anton Refregier. One of the largest WPA-era art projects, its 27 panels depict California life from the days when Indians were the state's sole inhabitants through World War I. Completion of this significant work was interrupted by World War II and political infighting; the latter led to some alteration in some of Refregier's "radical" historical interpretations. A permanent exhibit below the mural contains interesting photographs and artifacts of life in the Rincon area in the 1800s. Back in the mall, several new murals reflect San Francisco in the '90s—office workers at computers, sporting events, and the like.

Rincon Center represents the best aspects of the sometimes uneasy tension between preservationist forces and developers (and in this case the U.S. government). It took a fight to preserve the murals and the architecturally important post office, which now enhance what might otherwise be just another modern office space. The exhibit and the murals form a fascinating minimuseum, a 15-minute cultural and historical interlude for residents and tourists alike. The Historic Lobby is a modest example of something the city pioneered years ago: bringing art and history "to the people." The most visible of these programs are the large-scale permanent and temporary exhibits at the airport, among the first of their kind in the nation.

Two blocks farther south on Steuart Street is the newly restored **Hills Brothers Coffee** factory, now a retail and office complex. "Brew pubs," establishments that make their own suds right on the premises, are experiencing a new vogue in San Francisco. The **Gordon Biersch Brewing Co.,** also a restaurant, was an instant hit with local trendsetters. It's open for lunch and dinner.

Spear Street (parallel to Steuart on the other side of Rincon Center) leads back to Market Street. As you approach Market Street, your attention is drawn to the **Hyatt Regency Hotel** (Embarcadero 5), part of the huge **Embarcadero**

Center complex. The Hyatt, designed by John Portman, is noted for its spectacular lobby and 20-story hanging garden. On the waterfront side of the hotel is **Justin Herman Plaza.** There are arts and crafts shows, street musicians, and mimes here on weekends year-round. Kite flying is popular here. A huge concrete sculpture, the **Vaillancourt Fountain,** has had legions of critics since its installation in 1971; most of the time the fountain does not work, and many feel it is an eyesore.

A three-tier pedestrian mall connects the eight buildings that comprise Embarcadero Center. Frequently called "Rockefeller Center West," the complex includes more than 100 shops, 40 restaurants, and two hotels, as well as office and residential space. Louise Nevelson's dramatic 54-foot-high black-steel sculpture, *Sky Tree,* stands guard over Building 3.

Time Out | **Splendido's** (Embarcadero Center Four, tel. 415/986–3222) is a comfortable Mediterranean inn nestled amid the high rises. Its Italianate California cuisine, featuring fresh grilled meats and unusual marinades, has made this spot an instant classic. Lunch is the most popular meal here, and it is always very crowded, so try to reserve ahead. On a sunny day, it's fun to grab something to go at one of the dozen or so take-out shops and enjoy the goings-on in Justin Herman Plaza.

Those who find Vaillancourt Fountain unpalatably modern will perhaps relate better to the more classical **Donahue Monument,** which holds its own against the skyscrapers that tower over the intersection of Battery and Market streets. The work was designed by Douglas Tilden, a noted California sculptor who was deaf and dumb. A plaque below this homage to waterfront mechanics marks the spot as the location of the shoreline of San Francisco Bay in 1848.

Because it bisects the city at an angle, Market Street has consistently challenged San Francisco's architects over the years. At **388 Market** is a sleek, modern answer to the problem designed by Skidmore, Owings and Merrill. The block between Sutter and Post contains two

classic—and clever—solutions, Charles Ha-
vens's triangular **Flatiron Building** at 540–548
Market and Willis Polk's **Hobart Building** at 582
Market. The second building, considered to be
among Polk's best work in the city, is a gem. It's
worth the effort to walk south down Second
Street (which runs right into the building) to get
a full view of the Hobart tower's unique combination of a flat facade and oval sides.

On the north side of Market at the traffic island,
where Kearny, Third, and Geary streets come
together, is **Lotta's Fountain.** This quirky monument, which now goes largely unnoticed by local
passersby, was a gift to the city from singer
Lotta Crabtree, a Madonna prototype whose
"brash music hall exploits" were the talk of the
nation in the mid-1800s. Lotta designed the
fountain herself from a set in one of her shows.

From here, you can return to Union Square by
walking west on Geary. If you're still feeling
hearty and in a 19th-century frame of mind, continue up Market Street to Fifth. (Don't miss the
Wells Fargo Branch at Market and Grant, a
stately response to Market Street's oddly an-
gled ways.) Turn left at the San Francisco Shopping Centre and proceed to Mission Street. The
❷❻ Old San Francisco Mint, at 5th and Mission
streets, reopened as a museum in 1973. The century-old brick-and-stone building exhibits a
priceless collection of gold coins. Visitors tour
the vaults and can strike their own souvenir
medal on an 1869 press. *Tel. 415/744–6830. Admission free. Open weekdays 10–4.*

Tour 4: South of Market (SoMa)

The vast tract of downtown land south of Market
Street along the waterfront and west to the Mission district is now known by the acronym SoMa
(patterned after New York City's south-of-
Houston SoHo). Formerly known as South of the
Slot because of the cable-car slot that ran up
Market Street, the area has a history of housing
recent immigrants to the city—beginning with
tents set up in 1848 by the gold-rush miners and
continuing for decades. Except for a brief flowering of English-inspired elegance during the
mid-19th century in the pockets of South Park

and Rincon Hill, the area was reserved for new-comers who couldn't yet afford to move to anoth-er neighborhood. Industry took over most of the area when the big earthquake collapsed most of the homes into their quicksand bases.

Nearly 30 years ago, the San Francisco Redevel-opment Agency grabbed 87 acres of run-down downtown land, leveled anything that stood on them, and planned the largest building program in the city's history: **Yerba Buena Center.** The $1.5 billion project turned into something of a quagmire, proceeding in fits and starts through-out the '70s and '80s. After more than two dec-ades, it is finally beginning to take shape, although parts of it are still under construction and still other portions aren't past the blueprint stage.

For years industrial South of Market had been a stomping ground for alternative artists and the gay leather set. A dozen bars frequented by the latter group had existed alongside warehouses, small factories, and art studios. But the increas-ing visibility of gay culture, joined with redevel-opment fervor, gave South of Market a social sanction it hadn't had for 100 years. In the wake of the AIDS crisis, most of the area's gay bars have given way to trendy straight bars and most of the artists have repaired to cheaper ground. Within a few years, South of Market has been transformed into SoMa, a center for San Fran-cisco nightclubbing, dining, and gallery hop-ping. One other activity became popular in recent years: outlet shopping.

There are really two SoMas, one during the day and the other at night; one for businesspeople and bargain hunters, the other for the (mostly young) leisure class. The **Moscone Convention Center,** on Howard Street between 3rd and 4th streets, remains the centerpiece of the redevel-opment area. It is distinguished by a contempo-rary glass-and-girder lobby at street level (most of the exhibit space is underground) and a mono-lithic, column-free interior that was the site of the 1984 Democratic convention. In 1992, the center finished a $150 million expansion project that doubled its size and incorporated a new

building across Howard Street with underground exhibit space.

(28) Up 4th Street from the Moscone Convention
Center you can't miss the new **San Francisco
Marriott at Moscone Center** (777 Market St.),
the architectural curiosity that had the city in
an uproar when it opened in 1989. Its 40-story
ziggurat construction topped with reflecting
glass pinwheels elicited gasps from newspaper
columnists and passersby alike, earning it com-
parisons with a jukebox, a high-rise parking me-
ter, and a giant rectal thermometer. It takes its
civic place in a long line of blooper buildings in
the city that keep the city talking and passing
newer and newer building ordinances. Whether
San Franciscans will come to embrace the building—as they have the Transamerica pyramid—
is an open question; what's certain is that the hotel's 1,500 rooms already lure many of the city's
500,000 yearly visiting conventioneers. A bit of
history has been preserved next door to the
Marriott. The brick, Gothic Revival **St.
Patrick's Church** (756 Mission St.) was completed in 1872 and rebuilt after the 1906 earthquake and fire destroyed its interior.

Although the new San Francisco Museum of
Modern Art will soon anchor the SoMa art
scene, a number of specialized museums and
small galleries are already making important
contributions. Across 4th Street from the
Moscone Center is the **Ansel Adams Center.** This
gallery showcases historical and contemporary
photography, and has an extensive permanent
collection of Adams's work. *250 4th St., tel. 415/
495–7000. Admission: $4 adults, $3 students, $2
youths 12–17 and senior citizens, children under 12 free. Open Tues.–Sun. 11–5.*

Diagonally across Mission from the Marriott in
the Yerba Buena Gardens complex (the name
given to the block surrounded by 3rd, Mission,
(29) Howard and 4th streets) is the **Center for the
Arts** (706 Mission St., tel. 415/512–1000), which
opened in late 1993. The focus here is on the
multicultural arts—dance, music, performance,
theater, visual arts, film, video and installa-
tions—from the community-based to the international. The center includes two multi-use

theaters, three visual arts galleries, a film/video screening room, and an outdoor performance esplanade.

Three blocks south of the Center for the Arts on Third Street is the delightful **Cartoon Art Museum.** Rotating exhibits include comic books, plates and sketches from comic strips, animation cels, and computer-generated imagery. *665 3rd St. 5 fl., tel. 415/546–3922. Admission: $3 adults, $2 students, $1 senior citizens. Open Wed.–Fri. 11–5, Sat. 10–5. Sun. 1–5.*

Time Out   There are several fine restaurants in the area, but for atmosphere none of them can compare with **Hamburger Mary's.** (1582 Folsom St., tel. 415/626–5767). The decor is funky, the music loud, and the clientele polymorphous. Health food meets greasy spoon at Mary's: thick hamburgers are served on slices of nine-grain bread. For a more sedate repast, try the **Acorn** tea and griddle (1256 Folsom, tel. 415/863–2469), which serves lunch weekdays 11:30–2:30 and tea from 3–5.

Although many cleared out when urban renewal started in earnest, artists still hang out in SoMa and show their work in several galleries on the cutting edge of San Francisco's art scene. **Artspace** (1286 Folsom St., tel. 415/626–9100) operates more like a museum than a gallery, highlighting new artists in a not-for-sale setting. **New Langton Arts** (1246 Folsom St., tel. 415/626–5416) is one of the city's longest-surviving alternative exhibit and performance spaces. Its focus is mixed media and performance art, and it offers a provocative series of readings, music, and talks. The gallery may move in 1994, but will remain south of Market; call to be sure. **Eye Gallery** (1151 Mission St., tel. 415/431–6911) and **San Francisco Camerawork** (70 12th St., tel. 415/621–1001), as their names imply, turn the light on up-and-coming photographers.

The hottest area for nighttime entertainment south of Market is around 11th Street. **Club O,** formerly The Oasis (11th and Folsom Sts., tel. 415/621–8119), was the club that started luring straights back to a predominantly gay neighborhood, with its pool-on-the-premises parties and live music. Here's a twist: it's gay again one night (Thursday) a week. The **DNA Lounge** (375 11th St., tel. 415/626–1409) has a more aggressive new-wave attitude, and at the **Paradise Lounge** (11th and Folsom Sts., tel. 416/861–6906) you can catch such oddball specialty acts as chanteuse Connie Champagne and her Tiny Bubbles.

Slim's (333 11th St., tel. 415/621–3330) was opened by musician Boz Scaggs. Its focus is on "American roots" rock/rhythm-and-blues music; celebrity musicians, in town for gigs elsewhere, often drop by and occasionally sit in with the headliners.

Tour 5: Jackson Square

In the Gay Nineties San Francisco earned the title of "the Wickedest City in the World." The saloons, dance halls, cheap hotels, and brothels of its Barbary Coast attracted sailors and gold rushers. Most of this red-light district was destroyed in the 1906 fire; what remains is now ❸⓿ part of **Jackson Square**. A stroll through this district recalls some of the romance and rowdiness of early San Francisco.

Some of the city's earliest business buildings still stand in the blocks of Jackson Square between Montgomery and Sansome streets. By the end of World War II, most of the 1850 brick structures had fallen on hard times. In 1951, however, things changed. A group of talented, preservation-minded designers and furniture wholesale dealers selected the centrally located, depressed area for their showrooms. By the 1970s, the reclaimed two- and three-story renovated brick buildings were acclaimed nationwide. In 1972, the city officially designated the area—bordered by Columbus Avenue on the west, a line between Broadway and Pacific Avenue on the north, Washington on the south, and Sansome Street on the east—as San Francisco's first historic district. Seventeen buildings were given landmark status.

Jackson Square became the interior design center of the West. Unfortunately, property values soared, forcing many of the fabric and furniture outlets to move to the developing Potrero Hill section. Advertising agencies, attorneys, and antiques dealers now occupy the charming renovations.

The **Ghirardelli Chocolate Factory** was once housed at 415 Jackson. In 1857, Domenico Ghirardelli moved both his growing business and his family into this property. It was quite common for the upper floors of these buildings to be used as flats by either the building's owners or its tenants. By 1894, Ghirardelli had moved his expanding chocolate enterprise to Ghirardelli Square.

Another historic building is the former **A. P. Hotaling and Company whiskey distillery** at 451 Jackson. This handsome brick building retains the iron shutters installed in 1866 to "fireproof" the house. A plaque on the side of the building repeats a famous query about its surviving the quake: "If, as they say, God spanked the town/ for being overfrisky,/Why did He burn the churches down/and spare Hotaling's Whisky?"

Around the corner, south toward Washington, is the much-photographed compound at **722–28 Montgomery Street,** for years the headquarters of Melvin Belli, the "King of Torts," one of the nation's most flamboyant attorneys. The site was originally a warehouse and later the **Melodeon Theater,** where the immortal Lotta Crabtree (*see* Lotta's Fountain in Tour 3: The Embarcadero and Lower Market Street, *above*)

The **Golden Era Building** at 732 Montgomery Street also dates from the 1850s. It was the home of the most substantial literary periodical published locally during the 1850s and 1860s. Mark Twain and Bret Harte were two of its celebrated contributors.

Time Out Big windows, white walls, and chains of red peppers, garlic, and sausage set the stage for homemade pastas, charcoal-broiled seafood, and select wines, all of which make **Ciao** (230 Jackson St., tel. 415/982–9500) a special stop for lunch or dinner. Reservations are advised for dinner.

Tour 6: Chinatown

San Francisco is home to the largest Chinese community outside Asia. Although Chinese are visible throughout the city—a stretch of Clement Street in the Richmond district has become known as "New Chinatown"—bordered roughly by Bush, Kearny, Powell, and Broadway, this area remains the community's spiritual and political center. Recent immigrants from Southeast Asia have added new character and life to the neighborhood.

Visitors usually enter Chinatown through the green-tiled dragon-crowned **Chinatown Gate** at Bush Street and Grant Avenue. To best savor this district, explore it on foot (it's not far from Union Square), even though you may find the bustling, noisy, colorful stretches of Grant and Stockton streets north of Bush difficult to navigate. Parking is extremely hard to find, and traffic is impossible. As in Hong Kong, most families shop daily for fresh meats, vegetables, and bakery products. This street world shines with much good-luck crimson and gold; giant beribboned floral wreaths mark the opening of new bakeries, bazaars, and banks. Note the dragon-entwined lampposts, the pagoda roofs, and street signs with Chinese calligraphy.

Merely strolling through Chinatown and its many bazaars, restaurants, and curio shops yields endless pleasures, but you also have an opportunity here to experience a bit of one of the world's oldest cultures. You needn't be shy about stepping into a temple or an herb shop. Chinatown has been a tourist stop for more than 100 years now and most of its residents welcome "foreign" guests.

Dragon House Oriental Fine Arts and Antiques (455 Grant Ave.) is an excellent place to start your Chinatown visit. Its collection of ivory carvings, ceramics, and jewelry dates back 2,000 years and beyond. The shop's display window is a history lesson in itself.

San Francisco pioneered the resurrection of Chinese regional cooking for American palates. Cantonese cuisine, with its familiar staples of chow mein and chop suey (said to be invented in

San Francisco by gold rush–era Chinese cooks) now exists alongside spicier Szechuan, Hunan, and Mandarin specialties. With almost 100 restaurants squeezed into a 14-block area, Chinatown offers plenty of food. In the windows of markets on Stockton Street and Grant Avenue you can see roast ducks hanging, fresh fish and shellfish swimming in tanks, and strips of Chinese-style barbecued pork shining in pink glaze.

32 The handsome brick **Old St. Mary's Church** at Grant and California streets served as the city's Catholic cathedral until 1891. Granite quarried in China was used in the structure, which was dedicated in 1854. Diagonally across the inter-
33 section is **St. Mary's Park,** a tranquil setting for local sculptor Beniamino (Benny) Bufano's heroic stainless-steel androse-colored granite *Sun Yat-sen.* The 12-foot statue of the founder of the Republic of China was installed in 1937 on the site of the Chinese leader's favorite reading spot during his years of exile in San Francisco. Bufano was born in Rome on October 14, 1898, and died in San Francisco on August 16, 1970. His stainless-steel and mosaic statue of St. Francis welcomes guests at San Francisco International Airport.

The city's first house was built in 1836 at the corner of Grant Avenue and Clay Street; it was later destroyed in the 1906 earthquake. Turn right on Clay Street, continue one block to Kearny
34 Street, and turn left to reach **Portsmouth Square,** the potato patch that became the plaza for Yerba Buena. This is where Montgomery raised the American flag in 1846. Note the bronze galleon atop a nine-foot granite shaft. Designed by Bruce Porter, the sculpture was erected in 1919 in memory of Robert Louis Stevenson, who often visited the site during his 1879–80 residence. In the morning, the park is crowded with people performing solemn t'ai chi exercises. By noontime, dozens of men huddle around mahjongg tables, engaged in not always legal competition. Occasionally undercover police rush in to break things up, but this ritual, though as solemn as the t'ai chi, is hardly as productive.

㉟ From here you can walk to the **Chinese Cultural Center,** which frequently displays exhibits of Chinese-American artists as well as traveling exhibits of Chinese culture. The center also offers $12 Saturday-afternoon (2 PM) walking tours of historic points in Chinatown. *In the Holiday Inn, 750 Kearny St., tel. 415/986-1822. Admission free. Open Tues.-Sat. 10-4.*

㊱ In an alley parallel to and a half-block south of the side of the Holiday Inn, the **Chinese Historical Society** traces the history of Chinese immigrants and their contributions to the state's rail, mining, and fishing industries. *650 Commercial St., parallel to Clay St. off Kearny, tel. 415/391-1188. Admission free. Open Tues.-Sat. noon-4.*

㊲ The original Chinatown burned down after the 1906 earthquake; the first building to set the style for the new Chinatown is near Portsmouth Square, at 743 Washington Street. The three-tier pagoda called the **Old Chinese Telephone Exchange** (now the Bank of Canton) was built in 1909. The exchange's operators were renowned for their "tenacious memories," about which the San Francisco Chamber of Commerce boasted in 1914: "These girls respond all day with hardly a mistake to calls that are given (in English or one of five Chinese dialects) by the name of the subscriber instead of by his number—a mental feat that would be practically impossible to most high-schooled American misses."

㊳ **Buddha's Universal Church** is a five-story, hand-built temple decorated with murals and tile mosaics. *720 Washington St. Open 2nd and 4th Sun. of the month, 1-3.*

Time Out Skip that Big Mac you've been craving; opt instead for dim sum, a variety of pastries filled with meat, fish, and vegetables, the Chinese version of a smorgasbord. More than a dozen Chinese restaurants feature this unusual lunch/brunch adventure from about 11 AM to 3 PM. In most places, stacked food-service carts patrol the premises; customers select from the varied offerings, and the final bill is tabulated by the number of different saucers on the table. Dim sum restaurants tend to be big, crowded, noisy, cheap, and friendly. Suggestions are often offered by nearby strangers as to what is inside the tempting morsels. A favorite on Pacific Avenue, two blocks north of Washington Street, is **New Asia.** Many of the smaller, inexpensive Chinese restaurants and cafés do not accept credit cards; some serve beer and wine. *772 Pacific Ave., tel. 415/391-6666. Open for dim sum 8:30 AM-3 PM.*

Waverly Place is noted for ornate painted balconies and Chinese temples. **Tien Hou Temple** was dedicated to the Queen of the Heavens and Goddess of the Seven Seas by Day Ju, one of the first three Chinese to arrive in San Francisco in 1852. A sign in Chinese welcomes visitors (now you know). Climb three flights of stairs—past two mah-jongg parlors whose patrons hope the spirits above will favor them. As you enter the temple, elderly ladies are often preparing "money" to be burned as offerings to various Buddhist gods. A (real) dollar placed in the donation box on their table will bring a smile. Notice the wood carving suspended from the ceiling that depicts a number of gods at play. *125 Waverly Pl. Open daily 10 AM-4 PM.*

Throughout Chinatown you will notice herb shops that sell an array of Chinese medicines. The **Great China Herb Co.** (857 Washington St.), around the corner from the Tien Hou Temple, is one of the largest. All day, sellers fill prescriptions from local doctors, measuring exact amounts of tree roots, bark, flowers, and other ingredients with their hand scales, and add up the bill on an abacus. The shops also sell "over-the-counter" treatments for the common cold, heartburn, hangovers, and even impotence!

The other main thoroughfare in Chinatown, where locals shop for everyday needs, is Stockton Street, which parallels Grant Avenue. This is the real heart of Chinatown. Housewives jostle one another as they pick apart the sidewalk displays of Chinese vegetables. Double-parked trucks unloading crates of chickens or ducks add to the all-day traffic jams. You'll see excellent examples of Chinese architecture along this street. Most noteworthy is the elaborate **Chinese Six Companies** (843 Stockton St.), with its curved roof tiles and elaborate cornices. At 855 Stockton is **Kong Chow Temple,** established in 1851 and moved to this new building in 1977. Take the elevator up to the fourth floor. Again, a dollar bill is an appropriate gift from you or your group. The air at Kong Chow Temple is often thick with incense, a bit ironic what with the Chinese Community Smoke-Free Project but two floors below.

Around the corner at 965 Clay St. is the handsome, redbrick **Chinatown YWCA,** originally set up as a meeting place and residence for Chinese women in need of social services. It was designed by architect Julia Morgan, who was also responsible for the famous Hearst Castle at San Simeon, California. It's an easy half-hour walk back downtown to Union Square via the **Stockton Street Tunnel,** which runs from Sacramento Street to Sutter Street. Completed in 1914, this was the city's first tunnel to accommodate vehicular and pedestrian traffic.

Tour 7: North Beach and Telegraph Hill

Like neighboring Chinatown, North Beach, centered on Columbus Avenue north of Broadway, is best explored on foot. In the early days there truly was a beach. At the time of the gold rush, the bay extended into the hollow between Telegraph and Russian hills. North Beach, less than a square mile, is the most densely populated district in the city and is truly cosmopolitan. Much of the old-world ambience still lingers in this easygoing and polyglot neighborhood. Novelist Herbert Gold, a North Beach resident, calls the area "the longest running, most glorious American bohemian operetta outside Greenwich Village."

Like Chinatown, this is a section of the city where you can eat and eat. Restaurants, cafés, delis, and bakeries abound. Many Italian restaurants specialize in family-style full-course meals at reasonable prices. A local North Beach delicacy is focaccia—spongy pizzalike bread slathered with olive oil and chives or tomato sauce—sold fresh from the oven at quaint old **Liguria Bakery** at the corner of Stockton and Filbert streets. Eaten warm or cold, it is the perfect walking food.

Among the first immigrants to Yerba Buena during the early 1840s were young men from the northern provinces of Italy. By 1848, the village, renamed San Francisco, had become an overnight boomtown with the discovery of gold. Thousands more poured into the burgeoning area, seeking the golden dream. For many the trail ended in San Francisco. The Genoese started the still-active fishing industry, as well as much-needed produce businesses. Later the Sicilians emerged as leaders of the fishing fleets and eventually as proprietors of the seafood restaurants lining Fisherman's Wharf. Meanwhile, their Genoese cousins established banking and manufacturing empires.

42 **Washington Square** may well be the daytime social heart of what was once considered "Little Italy." By mid-morning, groups of conservatively dressed elderly Italian men are sunning and sighing at the state of their immediate world. Nearby, laughing Asian and Caucasian playmates race through the grass with Frisbees or colorful kites. Denim-clad mothers exchange shopping tips and ethnic recipes. Elderly Chinese matrons stare impassively at the passing parade. Camera-toting tourists focus their lenses on the adjacent Romanesque splendor of **43** **Sts. Peter and Paul,** often called the Italian Cathedral. Completed in 1924, its twin-turreted terra-cotta towers are local landmarks. On the first Sunday of October, the annual Blessing of the Fleet is celebrated with a mass followed by a parade to Fisherman's Wharf. Another popular annual event is the Columbus Day pageant.

The 1906 earthquake and fire devastated this area, and the park provided shelter for hundreds of the homeless. **Fior d'Italia,** facing the cathedral, is San Francisco's oldest Italian restaurant. The original opened in 1886 and continued to operate in a tent after the 1906 earthquake until new quarters were ready. Surrounding streets are packed with savory Italian delicatessens, bakeries, Chinese markets, coffeehouses, and ethnic restaurants. Wonderful aromas fill the air. (Coffee beans roasted at **Graffeo** at 733 Columbus Avenue are shipped to customers all over the United States.) Stop by the **Panelli Brothers deli** (1419 Stockton St.) for a memorable, reasonably priced meat-and-cheese sandwich to go. **Florence Ravioli Factory** (1412 Stockton St.) features garlic sausages, prosciutto, and mortadella, as well as 75 tasty cheeses and sandwiches to go. **Victoria** (1362 Stockton St.) has heavenly cream puffs and eclairs. Around the corner on Columbus Avenue is **Molinari's,** noted for the best salami in town and a mouth-watering array of salads.

South of Washington Square and just off Columbus Avenue is the **St. Francis of Assisi Church** (610 Vallejo St.). This 1860 Victorian Gothic building stands on the site of the frame parish church that served the gold-rush Catholic community.

Over the years, North Beach has attracted creative individualists. The Beat Renaissance of the 1950s was born, grew up, flourished, then faltered in this then-predominantly Italian enclave. The Beat gathering places are gone, and few of the original leaders remain. Poet Lawrence Ferlinghetti still holds court at his **City Lights Bookstore** (261 Columbus Ave.). The face of North Beach is changing. The bohemian community has migrated up Grant Avenue above Columbus Avenue. Originally called Calle de la Fundacion, Grant Avenue is the oldest street in the city. Each June a street fair is held on the upper part of the avenue, where a cluster of cafés, boutiques, and galleries attract crowds.

The view from Columbus and Broadway characterizes the crossroads at which the area finds itself. Chinatown encroaches on Broadway west of Columbus; on the east side of the street the self-proclaimed "birthplace of topless dancing," the Condor, is now a coffee shop. Up Columbus, moving away from the Financial District, the traditional North Beach mix of Italian restaurants and cafés remains. Southward, it's a mixed bag: skyscrapers loom overhead; although one of the earliest and shortest examples, the triangular Sentinel Building (916 Kearny St.), owned by movie-maker Francis Ford Coppola, is the one that grabs the eye.

Time Out   The richness of North Beach life-style is reflected in the neighborhood's numerous cafés. Breakfast at **Caffe Roma** (414 Columbus Ave.) and create your own omelet from a list of 11 ingredients. Skip the main room with its pastel murals of cherubs and settle at one of the umbrella-shaded tables on the patio. Francis Ford Coppola is a regular, and the adjoining **Millefiori Inn,** a charming bed-and-breakfast, frequently hosts film celebrities. Across the street is **Caffe Puccini** (411 Columbus Ave.). It could be Italy: Few of the staff speak English. Their caffe latte (coffee, chocolate, cinnamon, and steamed milk) and strains of Italian operas recall *Roman Holiday.* A Saturday morning must is around the corner at **Caffe Trieste** (601 Vallejo St.). Get there at about 11; at noon, the Giotta family's weekly musical begins. The program ranges from Italian pop and folk music to favorite family operas. The Trieste opened in 1956 and became headquarters for the area's beatnik poets, artists, and writers. **Caffe Malvina** (1600 Stockton St.), ideal for people-watching along Washington Square, started during the 1950s and was among the first U.S. importers of Italian-made espresso machines.

㊻   **Telegraph Hill** rises from the east end of Lombard Street to about 300 feet and is capped with the landmark Coit Tower, dedicated as a monument to the city's volunteer fire fighters. Early during the gold rush, an eight-year-old who would become one of the city's most memorable eccentrics, Lillie Hitchcock Coit, arrived on the scene. Legend relates that at age 17, "Miss Lil" deserted a wedding party and chased down the street after her favorite engine, Knickerbocker No. 5, clad in her bridesmaid finery. She was soon made an honorary member of the Knickerbocker Company, and after that always signed herself "Lillie Coit 5" in honor of her favorite fire engine. Lillie died in 1929 at the age of 86, leaving the city about $100,000 of her million-dollar-plus estate to "expend in an appropriate manner . . . to the beauty of San Francisco."

Telegraph Hill residents command some of the best views in the city, as well as the most difficult ascent to their aeries. The Greenwich stairs lead up to Coit Tower from Filbert Street, and there are steps down to Filbert Street on the opposite side of Telegraph Hill. Views are superb en route, but most visitors should either taxi up to the tower or take the Muni bus No. 39 Coit at Washington Square. To catch the bus from Union Square, walk to Stockton and Sutter streets, board the Muni No. 30, and ask for a transfer to use at Washington Square (Columbus Ave. and Union St.) to board the No. 39 Coit. Public parking is very limited at the tower, and on holidays and weekends there are long lines of cars and buses winding up the narrow road.

❹❼ Coit Tower stands as a monument not only to Lillie Coit and the city's fire fighters but also to the influence of the political radical Mexican muralist Diego Rivera. Fresco was Rivera's medium, and it was his style that unified the work of most of the 25 artists who painted the murals in the tower. The murals were commissioned by the U.S. government as a Public Works of Art Project. The artists were paid $38 a week. Some were fresh from art schools; others found no market for art in the dark depression days of the early 1930s. An illustrated brochure for sale in the tiny gift shop explains the various murals dedicated to the workers of California.

Ride the elevator to the top to enjoy the panoramic view of both the Bay Bridge and Golden Gate Bridge; directly offshore is the famous Alcatraz and just behind it, Angel Island, a hikers' and campers' paradise. There are often artists at work in Pioneer Park, at the foot of the tower. Small paintings of the scene are frequently offered for sale at modest prices. *Discoverer of America*, the impressive bronze statue of Christopher Columbus, was a gift of the local Italian community.

Walk down the Greenwich Steps to Montgomery Street, and turn right. At the corner where the Filbert Steps intersect, you'll find the Art Deco masterpiece at 1360 Montgomery Street. Its elegant etched-glass gazelle and palms counterpoint the silvered fresco of the heroic bridgeworker—echoed by an actual view of the Bay Bridge in the distance. Descend the Filbert Steps amid roses, fuchsias, irises, and trumpet flowers, courtesy of Grace Marchant, who labored for nearly 30 years to transform a dump into one of San Francisco's hidden treasures. At the last landing before the final descent to Sansome Street, pause and sit on the bench to breathe in the fragrance of roses as you gaze at the bridge and bay below.

At the foot of the hill you will come to the Levi Strauss headquarters, a carefully landscaped $150 million complex that appears so collegial and serene it is affectionately known as LSU (Levi Strauss University). Fountains and grassy knolls complement the stepped-back redbrick buildings and provide a stress-reducing environment perfect for brown-bag lunches.

Time Out You can choose the ingredients for an urban picnic at **Il Fornaio** (in the Plaza, 1265 Battery St., tel. 415/986–0100). The **Uno Poco di Tutti** deli offers a variety of cold pasta salads and such treats as giant artichokes stuffed with bread crumbs and capers. A bakery will provide you with Italian sweets, or you can eat in the dining room, choosing from the house specialties: meats from the rotisserie or pizzas from the oak-fired ovens.

Tour 8: Russian Hill

Just nine blocks or so from downtown, Russian Hill has long been home to old San Francisco families and, during the 1890s, to a group of bohemian artists and writers that included Charles Norris, George Sterling, and Maynard Dixon. An old legend says that during San Francisco's early days the steep hill (294 feet high) was the site of a cemetery for Russian seal hunters and traders. Now the hills are covered with an astounding array of housing: simple studios, sumptuous pied-à-terres, Victorian flats, and costly boxlike condos.

At Union Square, board the Powell-Mason cable car and hop off at Vallejo and Mason streets. This will put you at an ideal spot from which to photograph Alcatraz Island and the bay. Slowly start climbing the Vallejo Steps up to attractive

⑱ Ina Coolbrith Park. An Oakland librarian and poet, Ina introduced both Jack London and Isadora Duncan to the world of books. For years she entertained literary greats in her Macondray Lane home (near the park). In 1915, she was named poet laureate of California.

A number of buildings in this neighborhood survived the 1906 earthquake and fire and still stand today. The house at **1652–56 Taylor Street** was saved by alert fire fighters who spotted the American flag on the property and managed to quench the flames using seltzer water and wet sand. A number of brown-shingle structures on Vallejo Street designed by Willis Polk, one of the city's most famous architects, also survived. For years, the Polk family resided at **1013 Vallejo Street.** Stroll past **1034–1036 Vallejo**—both buildings, tucked in between new million-dollar condominium neighbors, were designed by Polk.

At this point, two secluded alleys beckon: To the north, **Russian Hill Place** has a row of Mediterranean-style town houses designed by Polk in 1915. On **Florence Place** to the south, 1920s stucco survivors reign over more contemporary construction.

Follow Vallejo Street west to Jones Street, turn right, and continue on to Green Street. The 1000 block of Green, on one of the three crests of Russian Hill, is one of the most remarkable blocks in

⑲ San Francisco. The **Feusier House** (1067 Green St.), built in 1857 and now a private residence, is one of two octagonal houses left in the city. On the other side of the street (at 1088) is the **1907 firehouse.** Local art patron Mrs. Ralph K. Davies bought it from the city in 1956. There is a small museum, and the property is often used for charity benefits.

Continue west on Green Street to Hyde Street, where the Hyde-Powell cable car line runs. Turn right and stroll up to Union Street. (If you're tired of walking, stop at the original Swensen's for an ice-cream treat.) At this point you have two options: You can meander down Union Street to Jones Street, turn right and walk a few

50 steps down to magical **Macondray Lane,** a quiet cobbled pedestrian street lined with Edwardian cottages. From a flight of steep wooden stairs that lead down to Taylor Street you'll get some spectacular views of the bay. From Taylor Street it is then a short walk downhill to North Beach.

51 Your other option is to keep walking north on Hyde Street three blocks to **Lombard Street.** Stretching the length of just one block, San Francisco's "crookedest street" drops down the east face of Russian Hill in eight switchbacks to Leavenworth Street. Few tourists with cars can resist the lure of the scary descent. Pedestrians should be alert while using the steep steps, especially when photographing the smashing views.

52 At the base of the steps, turn left on Leavenworth Street and then right on Chestnut Street. At 800 Chestnut Street is the **San Francisco Art Institute.** Established in 1871, it occupied the Mark Hopkins home at California and Mason streets from 1893 to 1906. The school carried on in temporary quarters until 1926, when the present Spanish Colonial building was erected on the top of Russian Hill. Be sure to see the impressive seven-section fresco painted in 1931 by the Mexican master Diego Rivera. There are also frequent exhibitions of student efforts.

From here you can walk back to Hyde Street and take the cable car back downtown or walk a few blocks north to the wharf. Hardy walkers will probably prefer to walk down to Columbus Avenue and then west on North Point or Beach streets to Ghirardelli Square, the Cannery, and Aquatic Park.

Tour 9: Nob Hill

If you don't mind climbing uphill, Nob Hill is within walking distance of Union Square. Once called the Hill of Golden Promise, it became Nob Hill during the 1870s when "the Big Four"— Charles Crocker, Leland Stanford, Mark Hopkins, and Collis Huntington—built their hilltop estates. It is still home to many of the city's elite as well as four of San Francisco's finest hotels.

In 1882 Robert Louis Stevenson called Nob Hill "the hill of palaces." But the 1906 earthquake and fire destroyed all the palatial mansions. The shell of one survived. The Flood brownstone (1000 California St.) was built by the Comstock silver baron in 1886 at a reputed cost of $1.5 million. In 1909 the property was purchased by the

53 prestigious **Pacific Union Club.** The 45-room exclusive club remains the bastion of the wealthy and powerful. Adjacent is a charming small park noted for its frequent art shows.

54 Neighboring **Grace Cathedral** (1051 Taylor St.) is the seat of the Episcopal church in San Francisco. The soaring Gothic structure took 53 years to build. The gilded bronze doors at the east entrance were taken from casts of Ghiberti's Gates of Paradise on the baptistery in Florence. The superb rose window is illuminated at night. There are often organ recitals on Sundays at 5 PM, as well as special programs during the holiday seasons.

55 The huge **Masonic Auditorium** (1111 California St.) is also the site of frequent musical events, including "Today's Artists," a concert series that highlights young classical musicians.

56 The **Cable Car Museum,** at the corner of Washington and Mason streets, exhibits photographs, old cars, and other memorabilia from the system's 115-year history. An overlook allows you to observe the cables that haul the city's cars in action. *Tel. 415/474–1887. Admission free. Open daily 10–5.*

Tour 10: Union Street

Union Street, west of Van Ness Avenue, was the first shopping street in San Francisco to renovate its gingerbread Victorians into trendy boutiques, galleries, and restaurants. Known colloquially as Cow Hollow because it was once a rural settlement with small farms, pastures, and resident dairy herds, the area is now known for great shopping, dining, and drinking.

To get to Union Street, take either Muni bus No. 45 from Sutter Street or bus No. 41 from North Beach's Washington Square. Get off at Gough Street and begin walking west. Note the histor-

57 ic **Octagon House** (2645 Gough St. at Union St.). It is one of the two remaining examples in the city of this mid-19th-century architectural form. The second landmark octagon is a private residence on Russian Hill. These two curious houses are all that is left locally of a national fad for eight-sided buildings that swept the country during the 1850s, inspired by a book written by a New York phrenologist, Orson S. Fowler. Eight-sided homes were thought to be good luck.

In 1953 the National Society of the Colony Dames of America purchased the Octagon House (built in 1861) for one dollar from the Pacific Gas & Electric Company. One condition stated that the structure had to be moved from its original site across the street at 2648 Gough Street. Today it serves as a museum and center for the society's activities. The house is a treasure trove of American antique furniture and accessories from the 18th and 19th centuries. *Admission free. Open Feb.–Dec., 2nd Sun. and 2nd and 4th Thurs. of each month noon–3.*

Time Out   On the 1900 block are two special eating spots. Try **Bepples** (1934 Union St.) for a fabulous pie-and-coffee break. **Perry's** (1944 Union St.) has long had a reputation as the singles bar and the crowds still flock here to see and be seen. It's also a popular all-day drop-in restaurant, and it serves a tasty hamburger.

58 The so-called **Wedding Houses** at 1980 Union Street were built during the late-1870s or 1880s. The romantic history of No. 1980 recounts that its builder, a dairy farmer named James Cudworth, sold the property to a father as wedding presents for his two daughters. In 1963 this property and the adjoining buildings were tastefully transformed from modest residences into charming flower-decked shops and cafés. Join some of San Francisco's young, rich, and trendy at **Prego** (2000 Union St.) and check out the latest in food and finery.

Meander west to Webster Street, make a right, **59** and continue down to the old **Vedanta Temple** (2963 Webster St.) at the corner of Filbert Street. This 1905 architectural cocktail may be the most unusual structure in San Francisco: It's a pastiche of Colonial, Queen Anne, Moorish, and Hindu opulence. Vedanta is the highest of the six Hindu systems of religious philosophy. One of its basic tenets is that all religions are paths to one goal.

If you care to check out still more fashionable shops, return to Union Street and continue on to Fillmore Street. Stroll north down Fillmore to Greenwich Street, where a number of small, fascinating shops have recently opened their doors. Two of the city's top dealers of Oriental art have settled here.

Tour 11: Pacific Heights

Pacific Heights forms an east–west ridge along the city's northern flank from Van Ness Avenue to the Presidio and from California Street to the bay. Some of the city's most expensive and dramatic real estate, including mansions and town houses priced at $1 million and up, are located here. Grand old Victorians, expensively face-lifted, grace tree-lined streets, although here and there glossy, glass-walled condo high rises obstruct the view.

Old money and some new, trade and diplomatic personnel, personalities in the limelight, and those who prefer absolute media anonymity occupy the city's most prestigious residential enclave. Few visitors see anything other than the pleasing facades of Queen Anne charmers, English Tudor imports, and Baroque bastions, but strolling can still be rewarding. As you walk through Pacific Heights, you'll notice that few of the structures feature adjoining gardens. Space has always been at a premium in San Francisco; only the city's richest residents could afford to purchase a lot and then not build. Even in wealthy Pacific Heights, many of the structures stand close together, but extend in a vertical direction for two or more stories.

A good place to begin a tour of the neighborhood is at the corner of Webster Street and Pacific Avenue, deep in the heart of the Heights. You can get here from Union Square by taking Muni Bus 3 from Sutter and Stockton to Jackson and

Fillmore streets. Head one block east on Jackson to Webster Street.

North on Webster Street, at 2550, is the massive Georgian brick mansion built in 1896 for William B. Bourn, who had inherited a Mother Lode gold mine. The architect, Willis Polk, was responsible for many of the most traditional and impressive commercial and private homes built from the prequake days until the early 1920s.

Neighbors include a consulate and, on the northwest corner, two classic showplaces. **2222 Broadway** is the three-story Italian Renaissance palace built by Comstock mine heir James Flood. Broadway uptown, unlike its North Beach stretch, is big league socially. The former Flood residence was given to a religious order. Ten years later, the Convent of the Sacred Heart purchased the Baroque brick Grant house (2220 Broadway) and both serve as school quarters today. A second top-drawer school, the Hamlin (2120 Broadway), occupies another Flood property.

Go east on Broadway and at the next corner turn right onto Buchanan Street, then left on Jackson Street to Laguna. The massive red sandstone **Whittier Mansion,** at 2090 Jackson Street, was one of the most elegant 19th-century houses in the state, built so solidly that only a chimney toppled over during the 1906 earthquake.

One block south on Laguna, at Washington Street, is **Lafayette Park,** a four-block-square oasis for sunbathers and dog-and-Frisbee teams. During the 1860s a tenacious squatter, Sam Holladay, built himself a big house of wood shipped round the Horn, in the center of the park. Holladay even instructed city gardeners as if the land were his own, and defied all attempts to remove him. The house was finally torn down in 1936.

Walking east on Washington street along the edge of Lafayette Park, the most imposing residence is the formal French **Spreckels Mansion** (2080 Washington St.). Sugar heir Adolph Spreckels's wife, Alma, was so pleased with her house that she commissioned architect George Applegarth to design the city's European museum, the California Palace of the Legion of Honor in Lincoln Park. Alma, one of the city's great iconoclasts, is the model for the bronze figure atop the Victory Monument in Union Square.

Continue east on Washington Street two more blocks to Franklin Street and turn left. At 2007 **(62)** Franklin is the handsome **Haas-Lilienthal Victorian.** Built in 1886, at an original cost of $18,000, this grand Queen Anne survived the 1906 earthquake and fire and is the only fully furnished Victorian open to the public. The carefully kept rooms offer an intriguing glimpse into turn-of-the-century taste and lifestyle. A small display of photographs on the bottom floor proves that this elaborate house was modest compared with some of the giants that fell to the fire. It is operated by the Foundation for San Francisco's Architectural Heritage. Tours of the house are given by docent volunteers two days a week. The volunteers also conduct an informative two-hour tour of the eastern portion of Pacific Heights on Sunday afternoons. *Tel. 415/441–3004. Admission: $4 adults, $2 senior citizens and children under 12. Open Wed. noon–3:30, Sun. 11–4:30. Pacific Heights tours ($3 adults, $1 seniors/children) leave the house Sun. at 12:30 PM.*

Going south on Franklin Street, don't be fooled by the neoclassical **Golden Gate Church** at 1901—what at first looks like a stone facade is actually redwood painted white. At 1735 **Franklin** is a stately brick Georgian that was built during the early 1900s for a coffee merchant. Looking east at the corner of Franklin Street and California is a "tapestry brick" **Christian Science church** built in the Tuscan Revival style. Its terra-cotta detailing is also noteworthy.

The **Coleman House** at 1701 Franklin Street is an impressive twin-turreted Queen Anne mansion built for a goldrush mining and lumber baron. At 1818 and 1834 California are two stunning **Italianate Victorians.** A block farther at 1990 California is the Victorian-era **Atherton House,** perhaps the oddest combination of architectural elements—among them Queen Anne and Stick-Eastlake—in all of Pacific Heights.

To return to downtown, walk up the side of the Atherton House to Sacramento and catch the No. 1 California bus (get a transfer and change to the No. 30 Stockton bus on Stockton Street). If you haven't ridden a cable car yet, disembark the No. 1 at Van Ness Avenue and walk one block south to the California line terminus. The wait here is much shorter than for the Powell-Hyde line.

If you'd like to see more Victorians, proceed west on California past the Atherton House another block to Laguna Street and turn left. The Italianate Victorians on the east side of the **1800 block** of Laguna Street cost only $2,000–$2,600 when they were built during the 1870s. This block is one of the most photographed rows of Victorians in the city.

Walk south on Laguna Street to Sutter and catch the No. 2, 3, or 4 buses to Union Square. Or proceed one block past Sutter to Post and walk west one block to Buchanan to begin the Japantown tour.

Tour 12: Japantown

Japanese-Americans began gravitating to the neighborhood known as the Western Addition prior to the 1906 earthquake. Early immigrants arrived about 1860, and they named San Francisco Soko. After the 1906 fire had destroyed wooden homes in other parts of the stricken city, many survivors settled in the Western Addition. By the 1930s the pioneers had opened shops, markets, meeting halls, and restaurants and established Shinto and Buddhist temples. Japantown was virtually disbanded during World War II when many of its residents, including second- and third-generation Americans, were "relocated" in camps.

Today **Japantown,** or "Nihonmachi," is centered on the slopes of Pacific Heights, north of Geary Boulevard, between Fillmore and Laguna streets. The Nihonmachi Cherry Blossom Festival is celebrated two weekends every April with a calendar of ethnic events. Walking in Nihonmachi is more than just a shopping and culinary treat; it is a cultural, sensory experience.

To reach Japantown from Union Square, take Munibus No. 38-Geary or No. 2, 3, or 4 on Sutter Street, westbound to Laguna. Remember to have exact change—fare is $1.

We recommend visiting Japantown and the Western Addition during the day. Though the hotel, restaurant, and Kabuki movie complex are relatively safe in the evenings, it is often difficult to avoid long waits at isolated bus stops or to find a cruising cab when you want to get back to the hotel. The proximity of the often-hostile street gangs in the Western Addition could cause unpleasant incidents.

The buildings around the traffic-free **Japan Center Mall** between Sutter and Post streets are of the shoji screen school of architecture, and Ruth Asawa's origami fountain sits in the middle. (*See* Tour 1: Union Square, *above*, for more information on Ms. Asawa.) The mall faces the three-block-long, five-acre **Japan Center.** In 1968, the multimillion-dollar development created by noted American architect Minoru Yamasaki opened with a three-day folk festival. The three-block cluster includes an 800-car public garage and shops and showrooms selling Japanese products: electronic products, cameras, tapes and records, porcelains, pearls, and paintings.

The center is dominated by its Peace Plaza and Pagoda located between the Tamasak Plaza and Kintetsu buildings. The original design of Professor Yoshiro Taniguchi of Tokyo, an authority on ancient Japanese buildings, has been altered greatly, mostly for the worse. Remaining from the original design are the graceful *yagura* (wooden drum tower) that spans the entrance to the mall and the copperroofed *Heiwa Dori* (Peace Walkway) between the Tamasak Plaza and Kintetsu buildings. The five-tier, 100-foot Peace Pagoda overlooks the plaza, where seasonal festivals are held. The pagoda draws on the tradition of miniature round pagodas dedicated to eternal peace by Empress Koken in Nara more than 1,200 years ago. It was designed by the Japanese architect Yoshiro Taniguchi "to convey the friendship and goodwill of the Japanese to the people of the United States." A cultural bridge modeled after Florence's Ponte Vecchio spans Webster Street, connecting the Kintetsu and Kinokuniya buildings.

Some 40 restaurants in the neighborhood feature a choice of Japanese, Chinese, or Korean food. Most are found in the mall, a few are on side streets, and the rest are in the center itself, concentrated on the "street of restaurants" in the Kintetsu Building. Following the practice in Japan, plastic replicas of the various dishes are on view.

If touring has about done you in, we suggest a brief respite at the **Kabuki Hot Springs** (1750 Geary Blvd.). Open daily, the communal bath is open for men only on Monday, Tuesday, Thursday, and Saturday, and for women only on Wednesday, Friday, and Sunday. The spa offers a number of steam, sauna, and massage packages. One, the Shogun, includes an hour of shiatsu massage. This method concentrates on pressure points in the body and is guaranteed to get you back on the track.

Time Out At a sushi bar, sample the bite-size portions of lightly seasoned rice and seaweed topped with various kinds of seafood, usually raw. Try to manage the chopsticks, dip (don't dunk) your portion into the soy sauce, and experience this typical Japanese favorite. Tea, sake, or excellent Japanese beer accompanies these morsels. One warning—the final bill is calculated by portion, and it is not unusual to run up a $20 tab per person. **Isobune,** on the second floor of the Kintetsu Building (tel. 415/563–1030), is unusual. The sushi chef prepares a variety of sushi, placing each small portion on a small wooden boat that floats on a "river" of water that circles the counter. The customer then fishes out a sampling. An inexpensive and popular snack are *ramen* (noodle dishes). The noodles are either boiled and served in a broth or prepared tossfried with bits of greens and meat added for flavor. The inexpensive but superb **Mifune,** diagonally across from Isobune, serves both hot and

cold noodles as well as either the fat strands of
udon noodles or the buckwheat soba.

Walk back east on Geary Boulevard to Gough
Street. This enclave of expensive high-rise residential towers is known as Cathedral Hill. Dra-
64 matic **St. Mary's Cathedral** was dedicated in
1971 at a cost of $7 million. The impressive Cath-
olic cathedral seats 2,500 people around the
central altar. Above the altar is a spectacular
cascade made of 7,000 aluminum ribs. Four magnificent stained-glass windows in the dome represent the four elements: the blue north
window, water; the light-colored south window,
the sun; the red west window, fire; and the
green east window, earth. Designed by a team
of local architects and Pier Nervi of Rome, the
Italian travertine church is approached through
spacious plazas.

Tour 13: Civic Center

San Francisco's Civic Center stands as one of
the country's great city, state, and federal
building complexes with handsome adjoining
cultural institutions. It's the realization of the
theories of turn-of-the-century proponents of
the "City Beautiful."

65 Facing Polk Street, between Grove and McAllister streets, **City Hall** is a French Renaissance
Revival masterpiece of granite and marble,
modeled after the Capitol in Washington. Its
dome is even higher than the Washington version, and it dominates the area. In front of the
building are formal gardens with fountains,
walkways, and seasonal flower beds. Brooks
Exhibit Hall was constructed under this plaza in
1958 to add space for the frequent trade shows
and other events based in the Bill Graham Civic
Auditorium, recently renamed in honor of the
late rock promoter, on Grove Street.

San Francisco's increasing numbers of homeless
people are often seen in the city's green spaces.
Visitors and residents should be aware of possible danger in strolling in park areas and deserted business sectors after dark.

66 Across the plaza from City Hall on Larkin
Street is the main branch of the **San Francisco**

Public Library. (A new library is being built around the corner; when the library is completed in 1995 this site will become the new Asian Art Museum.) History buffs should visit the San Francisco History Room and Archives on the third floor. Historic photographs, maps, and other memorabilia are carefully documented for the layman or research scholar. *Archives, tel. 415/557–4567. Open Tues., Wed., Fri. 1–6, Thurs. and Sat. 10–noon and 1–6.*

On the west side of City Hall, across Van Ness Avenue, are the Museum of Modern Art, the Opera House, and Davies Symphony Hall. The northernmost of the three is the Veterans' Building, whose third and fourth floors house the San Francisco **Museum of Modern Art.** (A new SFMOMA is under construction as part of the downtown Yerba Buena development, but this location will continue its exhibition programs through 1994). The museum's permanent collection was significantly enhanced in 1991 by the $40 million Haas bequest, which features Matisse's masterpiece, *Woman in a Hat,* as well as works by Derain, Manet, Monet, and Picasso. Traveling exhibitions bring important national and international paintings, photographs, graphics, and sculpture to the Bay Area. The Museum Store has a select offering of books, posters, cards, and crafts. The Museum Cafe serves light snacks as well as wine and beer. *At McAllister St. and Van Ness Ave., tel. 415/863–8800. Admission: $4 adults, $2 senior citizens and students 13 and over with ID; free for children under 13 and 1st Tues. of the month for all. Open Tues., Wed., Fri. 10–5, Thurs. 10–9, weekends 11–5. Closed major holidays.*

South of the Veteran's Building is the opulent **War Memorial Opera House,** which opened in 1932. Lotfi Mansouri has taken over as head of the San Francisco Opera, the largest opera company west of New York. Its regular season of world-class productions runs from September through December.

Time Out There are at least 40 restaurants within walking distance of the Civic Center. **Max's,** at 601 Van Ness Avenue in Opera Plaza, an upscale condo complex, serves such old-time favorites as lox and bagels and roast beef sandwiches as well as chicken Oriental salad, tortilla snacks, and tasty desserts. Don't be in a hurry: Service tends to be slow, especially on show nights (opera or symphony). Celebrity chef Jeremiah Tower's **Stars** (170 Redwood Alley, near Grove St. and Van Ness Ave.) offers exotic versions of California cuisine in an atmospheric room reminiscent of a Parisian bistro. For a quick pizza or a grilled chicken breast sandwich, dash across to **Spuntino** (524 Van Ness Ave.). Open until midnight on Friday and Saturday, this is an excellent spot for an after-theater cappuccino. No reservations.

South of Grove Street, still on Van Ness Avenue, is the $27.5 million home of the San Francisco **69** Symphony, the modern 3,000-plus-seat **Louise M. Davies Symphony Hall,** made of glass and granite. *Grove St. and Van Ness Ave., tel. 415/552–8338. Cost: $3 adults, $2 senior citizens and students. Tours of Davies Hall Wed. 1:30 and 2:30, Sat. 12:30 and 1:30. Tours of Davies Hall and the adjacent Performing Arts Center every half-hour Mon. 10–2.*

The **San Francisco Performing Arts Library and Museum,** also known as PALM, has as its mission to collect, document and preserve the San Francisco Bay Area's rich performing arts legacy. It houses the largest collection of its kind on the West Coast. Exhibitions often include programs, photographs, manuscripts, newspaper clippings, and other memorabilia of historic performance events. *399 Grove St., at Gough, tel. 415/255–4800. Admission free. Open Tues.– Fri. 10–5, Sat. noon–4.*

East of the Civic Center at Market and Fulton **70** streets, the **United Nations Plaza** is the site of a bustling farmers' market on Wednesday and Sunday.

Tour 14: The Northern Waterfront

Numbers in the margin correspond to points of interest on the Northern Waterfront: Tours 14– 15 map.

For the sight, sound, and smell of the sea, hop the Powell-Hyde cable car from Union Square to

the end of the line. From the cable car turnaround, Aquatic Park and the National Maritime
Museum are immediately to the west; Fort Mason, with its several interesting museums, is
just a bit farther west. If you're interested in exploring the more commercial attractions,
Ghirardelli Square is behind you and Fisherman's Wharf is to the east. We recommend casual clothes, good walking shoes, and a jacket or
sweater for mid-afternoon breezes or foggy
mists.

Or you could begin your day with one of the
early-morning boat tours that depart from
the Northern Waterfront piers. On a clear day
(almost always), the morning light casts a
warm glow on the colorful homes on Russian
Hill, the weather-aged fishing boats cluttered
at Fisherman's Wharf, rosy Ghirardelli Square
and its fairy-tale clock tower, and the swelling
seas beyond the entrance to the bay.

San Francisco is famous for the arts and crafts
that flourish on the streets. Each day more than
200 of the city's innovative jewelers, painters,
potters, photographers, and leather workers
offer their wares for sale. You'll find them at
Fisherman's Wharf, Union Square, Embarcadero Plaza, and Cliff House.

❶ The **National Maritime Museum** exhibits ship
models, photographs, maps, and other artifacts
chronicling the development of San Francisco
and the West Coast through maritime history.
*Aquatic Park, at the foot of Polk St., tel. 415/
556–8177. Admission free. Open daily 10–5, till
6 in summer.*

❷ The museum also includes the **Hyde Street Pier**
(two blocks east), where historic vessels are
moored. The highlight is the *Balclutha*, an 1886
full-rigged, three-mast sailing vessel that sailed
around Cape Horn 17 times. The *Eureka*, a side-
wheel ferry, and the *C.A. Thayer*, a three-
masted schooner, can also be boarded. *Tel. 415/
556–6435. Admission: $3 adults, children and
senior citizens free. Open fall–spring, daily
10–5; summer, daily 10–6.*

The *Pampanito,* at Pier 45, is a World War II
submarine. An audio tour has been installed.

Northern Waterfront: Tours 14–15

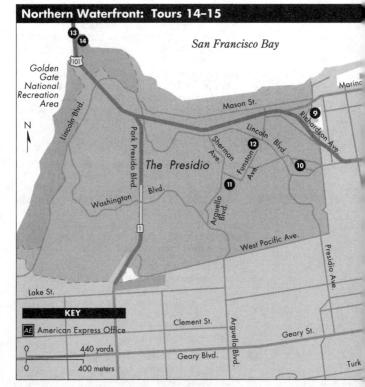

Buena Vista
Cafe, **6**

The Cannery, **5**

Fisherman's
Wharf, **7**

Fort Mason, **3**

Fort Point, **14**

Ghirardelli
Square, **4**

Golden Gate
Bridge, **13**

Hyde Street
Pier, **2**

National
Maritime
Museum, **1**

Officers'
Club, **11**

Palace of Fine
Arts, **9**

Pier 39, **8**

Presidio, **10**

Presidio Army
Museum, **12**

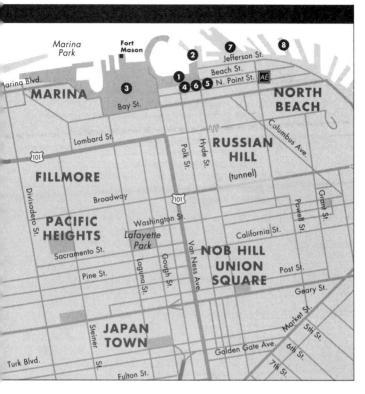

Marina
Park

**Fort
Mason**

❷

❼
Jefferson St.

❽

❶
Beach St.

MARINA

❸

Bay St.

❹ ❻ ❺ N. Point St. AE

**NORTH
BEACH**

Maring Blvd.

Columbus Ave.

Lombard St.

Hyde St.

Polk St.

**RUSSIAN
HILL**

(tunnel)

101

FILLMORE

Broadway

101

Powell St.

Grant St.

Divisadero St.

**PACIFIC
HEIGHTS**

Washington St.

*Lafayette
Park*

California St.

Sacramento St.

Laguna St.

Gough St.

Van Ness Ave.

**NOB HILL
UNION
SQUARE**

Post St.

Pine St.

Geary St.

Market St.

5th St.

**JAPAN
TOWN**

Steiner
St.

Golden Gate Ave.

6th St.

Turk Blvd.

Fulton St.

7th St.

*Tel. 415/929-0202. Admission: $4 adults, $2
senior citizens and students 12–18, $1 children
6–11 and active military. Open fall–spring,
Sun.–Thurs. 9–6, Fri.–Sat. 9–9; summer, daily 9–9.*

❸ **Fort Mason,** originally a depot for the shipment
of supplies to the Pacific during World War II, is
a 10-minute walk west from the back of the Maritime Museum. Follow the railway tracks in back
of the museum, turn right before they head into
a (blocked) tunnel and then left up the fairly
steep grade that leads to the complex. Fort Mason was converted into a cultural center in 1977.
The immense, three-story, yellow-stucco buildings are nondescript. Four minimuseums merit
mention, however.

The **Mexican Museum** was the first American
showcase to be devoted exclusively to Mexican
and Mexican-American art. Plans are underway
to build a larger modern building for the museum in the downtown Yerba Buena complex by
the late 1990s. The museum's goal is to expose
the vitality and scope of Mexican art from pre-
Hispanic Indian terracotta figures and Spanish
Colonial religious images to modern Mexican
masters. Limited space allows only a fraction of
the permanent collection, including a recent
500-piece folk-art collection (a gift from the Nel-
son A. Rockefeller estate), to be exhibited. The
museum recently began mounting major special
shows. One of the early, very successful exhibits
displayed the work of Frida Kahlo, the Mexican
surrealist and wife of Diego Rivera. The permanent collection includes such contemporary
greats as Rivera, Tamayo, Orozco, Siquieros,
and sculptor Francisco Zuniga. La Tienda, the
museum shop, stocks colorful Mexican folk art,
posters, books, and catalogues from museum
exhibitions. *Fort Mason, Bldg. D., tel. 415/441–
0404. Admission: $3 adults, $2 senior citizens
and students, children under 10 free; free admission noon–8 PM on the 1st Wed. of the month.
Open Wed.–Sun. noon–5.*

The **Museo Italo-Americano** has permanent exhibits of works of 19th- and 20th-century Ital-
ian-American artists. Shows include paintings,
sculpture, etchings, and photographs. The mu-

seum presents special exhibits, lectures, and films. *Fort Mason, Bldg. C, tel. 415/673–2200. Admission: $2 adults, $1 senior citizens and students. Open Wed.–Sun. noon–5.*

The **San Francisco African-American Historical and Cultural Society** maintains the only black museum west of the Rockies. The permanent collection includes exhibits on black California and black Civil War history. Temporary exhibits focus on living California black artists. *Fort Mason, Bldg. C, Room 165, tel. 415/441–0640. Admission: $1 adults, 75¢ teens 13–17, 50¢ children under 12. Open Wed.–Sun. noon–5. Phone to verify schedules.*

The **San Francisco Craft and Folk Art Museum** features American folk art, tribal art, and contemporary crafts. *Fort Mason, Bldg. A, tel. 415/ 775–0990. Admission: $1 adults, 50¢ senior citizens and children; admission free Sat. 10– noon. Open Tues.–Sun. 11–5, Sat. 10–5.*

Several theater companies are housed at Fort Mason. Of particular note is the **Magic Theatre** (Fort Mason, Bldg. D, tel. 415/441–8822), known for producing the works of such contemporary playwrights as Sam Shepard and Michael McClure.

The SS *Jeremiah O'Brien* is a World War II Liberty Ship freighter. The ship is staffed by volunteers, and there are special "steaming weekends," when the steam engine is in operation, the coal stove galley is open, and the "Slop Chest" store is set up. This is usually the third weekend of the month, but call to verify. *Fort Mason, Pier 3 East, Marina Blvd. and Buchanan St., tel. 415/441–3101. Admission: $2 adults, $1 children and senior citizens, $5 per family. Admission on steaming weekends: $3 adults, $1 children and senior citizens, $6 per family. Open weekdays 9–3, weekends 9–4.*

Time Out The San Francisco Zen Center operates a famous and beautiful restaurant at Fort Mason. **Greens** (Fort Mason, Bldg. A, tel. 415/771–6222) has won international acclaim for its innovative vegetarian menu. The room is decorated with contemporary art and offers some of the finest views (from down close to the water) across the bay to the Golden Gate Bridge. Reservations are essential, but you can stop by the bakery during the day and pick up some of their famous bread and pastries.

❹ Spend some time strolling through **Ghirardelli Square,** which is across Beach Street from the National Maritime Museum. This charming complex of 19th-century brick factory buildings has been transformed into specialty shops, cafés, restaurants, and galleries. Until the early 1960s, the Ghirardelli Chocolate Company's aromatic production perfumed the Northern Waterfront. Two unusual shops deserve mention: **Xanadu Gallery** and the adjoining **Folk Art International** display museum-quality tribal art from Asia, Africa, Oceania, and the Americas. Xanadu's array of antique and ethnic jewelry is peerless. For a musical interlude, poke an ear into **Richter's Music Boxes,** which carries superb examples of the craft from Switzerland and elsewhere.

❺ Just east of the Hyde Street Pier, **The Cannery** is a three-story structure built in 1894 to house what became the Del Monte Fruit and Vegetable Cannery. Shops, art galleries, and unusual restaurants ring the courtyard today, and the new **Museum of the City of San Francisco** can be found on the third floor. The first independent museum on the history of the city displays a number of significant historical items, maps, and photographs, including the eight-ton head of the Goddess of Progress statue that toppled from City Hall just before the 1906 earthquake. *2801 Leavenworth St., tel. 415/928–0289. Admission free. Open Wed.–Sun. 10–4.*

Just across the street, additional shopping and snacking choices are offered at the flag-festooned **Anchorage mall.**

❻ The mellow **Buena Vista Cafe** (2765 Hyde St.) claims to be the birthplace of Irish Coffee Stateside; the late San Francisco columnist Stan Delaplane is credited with importing the Gaelic concoction. The BV opens at 9 AM, serving a great breakfast. It is always crowded; try for a table overlooking nostalgic Victorian Park with its cable-car turntable.

7 A bit farther down at Taylor and Jefferson streets is **Fisherman's Wharf.** Numerous seafood restaurants are located here, as well as sidewalk crab pots and counters that offer takeaway shrimp and crab cocktails. Ships creak at their moorings; sea gulls cry out for a handout. By mid-afternoon, the fishing fleet is back to port. T-shirts and sweats, gold chains galore, redwood furniture, acres of artwork—some original—beckon visitors. Wax museums, fast-food favorites, amusing street artists, and the animated robots at Lazer Maze provide diversions for all ages.

Time Out A great family spot on the wharf is **Bobby Rubino's** (245 Jefferson St.). Barbecued ribs, shrimp, chicken, and burgers—there is something tasty for everyone. A favorite with couples is crowded, noisy **Houlihan's** at the Anchorage mall. It is noted for fancy drinks, fantastic bay views, tasty pizza and pastas, plus nightly music and dancing.

Today's tourists daily have the opportunity of enjoying exhilarating cruising on the bay. Among the cruises of the **Red and White Fleet,** berthed at Pier 41, are frequent 45-minute swings under the Golden Gate Bridge and the Northern Waterfront. Cruises and tours are also available to Sausalito, Angel Island, Muir Woods, Marine World Africa USA, and the Napa Valley Wine Country. Advanced reservations, even in the off-season, are strongly recommended for the very popular Alcatraz Island tour, which enables passengers to take a self-guided tour through the prison and grounds. *Alcatraz tours: $5.50 adults, $4.60 senior citizens and children 12–18, $3 for children; for audio tour, add $3 for adults, seniors, and children 12–18, $1 for children 5–11. Add $2 per ticket to charge by phone at 415/546–2700. Bay Cruises: $15 for adults, $12 for senior citizens and children 12–18, $8 children 5–11 (audio included).*

The **Blue and Gold Fleet,** berthed at Pier 39, provides its passengers with validated parking across the street. The 1¼-hour tour sails under both the Bay and Golden Gate bridges. Dinner-dance cruises run April–mid-December. *Tel. 415/781–7877. Reservations not necessary. Bay Cruise: $14 adults, $7 senior citizens, active military, and children 5–18, under 5 free. Summertime dinner-dance cruise: $35 per person (group rates available). Daily departures.*

8 **Pier 39** is the most popular of San Francisco's waterfront attractions, drawing millions of visitors each year to browse through its dozens of shops. Check out The Disney Store, with more Mickey Mouses than you can shake a stick at; Left Hand World, where left-handers will find all manner of gadgets designed with lefties in mind; and Only in San Francisco, the place for San Francisco memorabilia and the location of the Pier 39 information center. Ongoing free entertainment, accessible validated parking, and nearby public transportation ensure crowds most days. Don't miss the hundreds of sea lions that bask and play on the docks on the pier's north side. Bring a camera.

Tour 15: The Marina and the Presidio

9 San Francisco's rosy and Rococo **Palace of Fine Arts** is at the very end of the Marina, near the intersection of Baker and Beach streets. The palace is the sole survivor of the 32 tinted plaster structures built for the 1915 Panama-Pacific Exposition. Bernard Maybeck designed the Roman Classic beauty, and in the ensuing 50 years the building fell into disrepair. It was reconstructed in concrete at a cost of $7 million and reopened in 1967, thanks to legions of sentimental citizens and a huge private donation that saved the palace from demolition. The massive columns, great rotunda, and swan-filled lagoon will be familiar from fashion layouts as well as from many recent films. Recently, travelers on package tours from Japan have been using it as a backdrop for wedding-party photos, with the brides wearing Western-style finery.

The interior houses a fascinating hands-on museum, the **Exploratorium.** It has been called the best science museum in the world. The curious of all ages flock here to try to use and understand some of the 600 exhibits. Be sure to include the pitch-black, crawl-through Tactile

Dome in your visit. *Tel. 415/563-7337 or 415/
563-0362 for required reservations for Tactile
Dome. Admission: $8 adults, $6 students over
18 w/ID, $4 children 6-17. Open Tues.-Sun.
10-5, Wed. 10-9:30, legal Mon. holidays 10-5.*

If you have a car, now is the time to use it for a
⑩ drive through the **Presidio.** (If not, Muni bus No.
38 from Union Square will take you to Park Presidio; from there use a free transfer to bus No.
28 into the Presidio.) A military post for more
than 200 years, this headquarters of the U.S.
Sixth Army may soon become a public park. De
Anza and a band of Spanish settlers claimed the
area in 1776. It became a Mexican garrison in
1822 when Mexico gained its independence from
Spain. U.S. troops forcibly occupied it in 1846.

The more than 1,500 acres of rolling hills, majestic woods, and attractive redbrick army bar-
racks present an air of serenity in the middle of
the city. There are two beaches, a golf course,
⑪ and picnic sites. The **Officers' Club,** a long, low
adobe, was the Spanish commandante's headquarters, built about 1776, and is the oldest
⑫ standing building in the city. The **Presidio Army
Museum** is housed in the former hospital and focuses on the role played by the military in San
Francisco's development. *On the corner of Lincoln Blvd. and Funston Ave., tel. 415/561-4115.
Admission free. Open Tues.-Sun. 10-4.*

⑬ Muni bus No. 28 will take you to the **Golden Gate
Bridge** toll plaza. San Francisco celebrated the
50th birthday of the orange suspension bridge
in 1987. Nearly 2 miles long, connecting San
Francisco with Marin County, its Art Deco design is powerful, serene, and tough, made to
withstand winds of over 100 miles per hour.
Though frequently gusty and misty (walkers
should wear warm clothing), the bridge offers
unparalleled views of the Bay Area. The east
walkway offers a glimpse of the San Francisco
skyline as well as the islands of the bay. On a
sunny day sailboats dot the water, and brave
windsurfers test the often treacherous tides be-
neath the bridge. The view west confronts you
with the wild hills of the Marin headlands, the
curving coast south to Lands End, and the majestic Pacific Ocean. There's a vista point on the

Marin side, where you can contemplate the city and its spectacular setting.

⑭ **Fort Point** was constructed during the years 1853–1861 to protect San Francisco from sea attack during the Civil War. It was designed to mount 126 cannons with a range of up to 2 miles. Standing under the shadow of the Golden Gate Bridge, the national historic site is now a museum filled with military memorabilia. Guided group tours are offered by National Park Rangers, and there are cannon demonstrations. There is a superb view of the bay from the top floor. *Tel. 415/556–1693. Admission free. Open Wed.–Sun. 10–5.*

From here, hardy walkers may elect to stroll about 3½ miles (with bay views) along the Golden Gate Promenade to Aquatic Park and the Hyde Street cable car terminus.

Tour 16: Golden Gate Park

It was a Scotsman, John McLaren, who became manager of Golden Gate Park in 1887 and transformed the brush and sand into the green civilized wilderness we enjoy today. Here you can attend a polo game or a Sunday band concert and rent a bike, boat, or roller skates. On Sundays, some park roads are closed to cars and come alive with joggers, bicyclists, skaters, museum goers, and picnickers. There are tennis courts, baseball diamonds, soccer fields, and a buffalo paddock, and miles of trails for horseback riding in this 1,000-acre park.

Because it is so large, the best way for most visitors to see it is by car. Muni buses provide service, though on weekends there may be a long wait. On Market Street, board a westbound No. 5-Fulton or No. 21-Hayes bus and continue to Arguello and Fulton streets. Walk south about 500 feet to John F. Kennedy Drive.

From May through October, free guided walking tours of the park are offered every weekend by the Friends of Recreation and Parks (tel. 415/221–1311).

The oldest building in the park and perhaps San Francisco's most elaborate Victorian is the **Conservatory,** a copy of London's famous Kew Gardens. The ornate greenhouse was originally brought around the Horn for the estate of James Lick in San Jose. The Conservatory was purchased from the Lick estate with public subscription funds and erected in the park. In addition to a tropical garden, there are seasonal displays of flowers and plants and a permanent exhibit of rare orchids. *Admission: $1.50 adults, 75¢ seniors and children 6–12, children under 6 and last half-hour free. Open daily 9–5.*

The eastern section of the park has three museums. Purchase of a $10 Golden Gate Park Cultural Pass gains you one-day admission to all three, plus the Japanese Tea Garden and the Conservatory, a substantial savings (for adults) if you are planning to visit all these attractions. Purchase your pass at any of the museums or at TIX Bay Area in Union Square. **M. H. de Young Memorial Museum** was completely reorganized in 1989. It now features American art, with collections of painting, sculpture, textiles, and decorative arts from Colonial times through the 20th century. Fifteen new galleries highlight the work of American masters, including Copley, Eakins, Bingham, and Sargent. Don't miss the room of landscapes, dominated by Frederic Church's moody, almost psychedelic *Rainy Season in the Tropics*. There is a wonderful gallery of American still-life and trompe l'oeil art and a small selection of classic Shaker furniture. The de Young has also retained its dramatic collection of tribal art from Africa, Oceania, and the Americas, which includes pottery, basketry, sculpture, and ritual clothing and accessories. In addition to its permanent collections, the museum hosts selected traveling shows—often blockbuster events for which there are long lines and additional admission charges.

The museum has an outstanding shop with a wide selection of art objects. The **Cafe de Young,** which has outdoor seating in the Oakes Garden, serves a complete menu of light refreshments until 4 PM. *Tel. 415/863–3330 for 24-hr information. Admission: $5 adults, $3 senior citizens, $2 youths 12–17, under 12 free; free 1st Wed. and Sat. morning of the month. Note: 1 admission charge admits you to the de Young, Asian Art,*

*and Legion of Honor museums on the same day.
Open Wed. 10–8:45, Thurs.–Sun. 10–5.*

The **Asian Art Museum** is located in galleries
that adjoin the de Young. This world-famous
Avery Brundage collection consists of more
than 10,000 sculptures, paintings, and ceramics
that illustrate major periods of Asian art. Very
special are the Magnin Jade Room and the
Leventritt collection of blue and white porcelains. On the second floor are treasures from
Iran, Turkey, Syria, India, Tibet, Nepal, Paki-
stan, Korea, Japan, Afghanistan, and Southeast
Asia. Both the de Young and Asian Art museums have daily docent tours. *Tel. 415/668–8921.
Admission collected when entering the de
Young. Open Wed. 10–8:45, Thurs.–Sun. 10–5.*

Time Out The **Japanese Tea Garden,** next to the Asian Art
Museum, is ideal for resting after museum tour-
ing. This charming four-acre village was created
for the 1894 Mid-Winter Exposition. Small
ponds, streams, and flowering shrubs create a
serene landscape. The cherry blossoms in
spring are exquisite. The Tea House (tea, of
course, and cookies are served) is popular and
busy. *Tel. 415/752–1171. Admission: $2 adults,
$1 senior residents of San Francisco and chil-
dren 6–12. Open daily 8:30–6:30. Gates close at
5:30 in the summer, earlier in winter months.*

The **California Academy of Sciences** is directly
opposite the de Young Museum. It is one of the
five top natural history museums in the country
and has both an aquarium and a planetarium.
Throngs of visitors enjoy its Steinhart Aquarium, with its dramatic 100,000-gallon Fish
Roundabout, home to 14,000 creatures, and a
living coral reef with colorful fish, giant clams,
tropical sharks, and a rainbow of hard and soft
corals. There is an additional charge for Morri-
son Planetarium shows ($2.50 adults, $1.25 senior citizens and students, tel. 415/750–7138 for
daily schedule). The Space and Earth Hall has
an "earthquake floor" that enables visitors to
ride a simulated California earthquake. The
Wattis Hall of Man presents lifelike habitat
scenes that range from the icy terrain of the arc-
tic Inuit to the lush highlands of New Guinea.

Newly renovated is the Wild California Hall, with a 10,000-gallon aquarium tank showing underwater life at the Farallones (islands off the coast of northern California), life-size elephant seal models, and video information on the wildlife of the state. The innovative Life through Time Hall tells the story of evolution from the beginnings of the universe through the age of dinosaurs to the age of mammals. A cafeteria is open daily until one hour before the museum closes. The Academy Store offers a wide selection of books, posters, toys, and cultural artifacts. *Tel. 415/750-7145. Admission: $6 adults, $3 senior citizens and students 12-17, $1 children 6-11. $2 discount with Muni transfer. Free 1st Wed. of each month. Open July 4-Labor Day, daily 10-7; Labor Day-July, daily 10-5.*

A short stroll from the Academy of Sciences will take you to the free **Shakespeare Garden.** Two hundred flowers mentioned by the Bard, as well as bronze-engraved panels with floral quotations, are set throughout the garden.

Strybing Arboretum specializes in plants from areas with climates similar to that of the Bay Area, such as the west coast of Australia, South Africa, and the Mediterranean. There are many gardens inside the grounds, with 6,000 plants and tree varieties blooming seasonally. *9th Ave. at Lincoln Way, tel. 415/661-0668. Admission free. Open weekdays 8-4:30, weekends and holidays 10-5. Tours leave the bookstore weekdays at 1:30 PM, weekends at 10:30 AM and 1:30 PM.*

The western half of Golden Gate Park offers miles of wooded greenery and open spaces for all types of spectator and participant sports. Rent a paddleboat or stroll around **Stow Lake.** The Chinese Pavilion, a gift from the city of Taipei, was shipped in 6,000 pieces and assembled on the shore of Strawberry Hill Island in Stow Lake in 1981. At the very western end of the park, where Kennedy Drive meets the Great Highway, is the beautifully restored 1902 **Dutch Windmill** and the photogenic **Queen Wilhelmina Tulip Garden.**

Tour 17: Lincoln Park and the Western Shoreline

No other American city provides such close-up viewing of the power and fury of the surf attacking the shore. From Land's End in Lincoln Park you can look across the Golden Gate (the name was originally given to the opening of San Francisco Bay long before the bridge was built) to the Marin Headlands. From Cliff House south to the San Francisco Zoo, the Great Highway and Ocean Beach run along the western edge of the city.

The wind is often strong along the shoreline, summer fog can blanket the ocean beaches, and the water is cold and usually too rough for swimming. Carry a sweater or jacket and bring binoculars.

At the northwest corner of the San Francisco Peninsula is **Lincoln Park.** At one time all the city's cemeteries were here, segregated by nationality. Today there is an 18-hole golf course with large and well-formed Monterey cypresses lining the fairways. There are scenic walks throughout the 275-acre park, with particularly good views from **Land's End** (the parking lot is at the end of El Camino del Mar). The trails out to Land's End, however, are for skilled hikers only: There are frequent landslides, and danger lurks along the steep cliffs.

Also in Lincoln Park is the **California Palace of the Legion of Honor.** The building itself—modeled after the 18th-century Parisian original—is architecturally interesting and spectacularly situated on cliffs overlooking the ocean and the Golden Gate Bridge. The museum closed in 1992 for what is scheduled to be a two-year renovation, and is set to reopen in late 1994.

Cliff House (1066 Point Lobos Ave.), where the road turns south along the western shore, has existed in several incarnations. The original, built in 1863, and several later structures were destroyed by fire. The present building has restaurants, a pub, and a gift shop. The lower dining room overlooks **Seal Rocks** (the barking marine mammals sunning themselves are actually sea lions).

An adjacent (free) attraction is the **Musée Mécanique,** a collection of antique mechanical contrivances, including peep shows and nickelodeons. The museum carries on the tradition of arcade amusement at the Cliff House. *Tel. 415/ 386–1170. Open weekdays 11–7, weekends 10–7.*

Two flights below Cliff House is a fine observation deck and the Golden Gate National Recreation Area **Visitors Center.** There are interesting and historic photographs of Cliff House and the glass-roofed Sutro Baths. The baths covered three acres just north of Cliff House and comprised six enormous baths, 500 dressing rooms, and several restaurants. The baths were closed in 1952 and burned in 1966. You can explore the ruins on your own (the Visitors Center offers information on these and other trails) or take ranger-led walks on weekends. *Tel. 415/556– 8642. Open daily 10–4:30.*

Because traffic is often heavy in summer and on weekends, you might want to take the Muni system from the Union Square area out to Cliff House. On weekdays, take the Muni No. 38-Geary Limited to 48th Avenue and Point Lobos and walk down the hill. (On weekends and during the evenings, the Muni No. 38 is marked 48th Avenue. Don't take the No. 38 bus marked "Ocean Beach," though, or you'll have to walk an extra 10 minutes to get to the Cliff House.)

Below the Cliff House are the **Great Highway** and **Ocean Beach.** Stretching for 3 miles along the western (Pacific) side of the city, this is a beautiful beach for walking, running, or lying in the sun—but not for swimming. Although dozens of surfers head to Ocean Beach each day, you'll notice they are dressed head-to-toe in wet suits, as the water here is extremely cold. Across the highway from the beach is a new path, which winds through landscaped sand dunes from Lincoln Avenue to Sloat Boulevard (near the zoo)—an ideal route for walking and bicycling.

At the Great Highway and Sloat Boulevard is the **San Francisco Zoo.** The zoo was begun in 1889 in Golden Gate Park. At its present home there are 1,000 species of birds and animals, more than 130 of which have been designated endangered species. Among the protected are the snow leopard, Sumatran tiger, red panda, jaguar, and the Asian elephant. A favorite attraction is the greater one-horned rhino, next to the African elephants.

Gorilla World, a $2 million exhibit, is one of the largest and most natural gorilla habitats in a zoo. The circular outer area is carpeted with natural African Kikuyu grass, while trees, shrubs, and waterfalls create communal play areas. The $5 million Primate Discovery Center houses 16 endangered species in atriumlike enclosures. One of the most popular zoo residents is Prince Charles, a rare white tiger and the first of its kind to be exhibited in the West.

There are 33 "storyboxes" throughout the zoo that when turned on with the blue plastic elephant keys ($1.50) recite animal facts and basic zoological concepts in four languages (English, Spanish, Cantonese, and Tagalog).

The children's zoo has a minipopulation of about 300 mammals, birds, and reptiles, plus an insect zoo, a baby animal nursery, and a beautifully restored 1921 Dentzel Carousel. A ride astride one of the 52 hand-carved menagerie animals costs 75¢.

Zoo information, tel. 415/753–7083. Admission: $6.50 adults, $3 youths 12–15 and senior citizens, $1 children 6–12, under 5 free when accompanied by an adult; free 1st Wed. of the month. Open daily 10–5. Children's zoo admission: $1, under 3 free. Open daily 11–4.

Tour 18: The Mission District

Numbers in the margin correspond to points of interest on the Mission District and Castro Street: Tours 18–19 map.

During the 19th century the sunny weather of the then-rural Mission District made it a popular locale for resorts, racetracks, and gambling places. At 13th and Mission streets, where freeway traffic now roars overhead, stood Woodward's Gardens, a lush botanical garden with a zoo, playground, and pavilions featuring acrobatic performances.

Mission Street is the commercial center of the district, and all the resident ethnic cultures are reflected in the businesses: Spanish-language theaters, Italian restaurants, Arab-owned clothing stores, Vietnamese markets, and Filipino, Hispanic, and Chinese restaurants and groceries. The majority of Latinos here are from Central America. Most of them settled here during the late 1960s and early 1970s; many of them are now service workers. The Mexican-Americans are a minority of the estimated 50,000 Hispanics in the Mission.

① **Mission Dolores,** on palm-lined Dolores Street, is the sixth of the 21 missions founded by Father Junipero Serra. The adobe building was begun in 1782 and was originally known as Mission San Francisco de Assisi. Completed in 1791, its ceiling depicts original Costanoan Indian basket designs, executed in vegetable dyes. There is a small museum, and the mission cemetery contains the graves of more than 5,000 Indians. *Dolores and 16th Sts., tel. 415/621–8203. Admission: $1. Open daily 9–4.*

② The nearby **Dolores Park** (Dolores St. between 18th and 20th Sts.) offers dramatic views of the high rises of downtown as a backdrop for the pastel bay-windowed Mission District houses. Drug activity has made the park less safe in recent years.

Two blocks from Mission Dolores, the area around 16th and Valencia streets is developing its own neighborhood character. A mix of socialists, lesbian-feminists, new wavers, and traditional Hispanics has made it San Francisco's **③** new bohemia. The **Roxie Cinema** (3117 16th St., tel. 415/863–1087) is an aggressive showcase for independent films. Across the street, **Cafe Picaro** (3120 16th St.) appears to be a leftover from the '60s. People gather here for political discussions and to work on papers, read books, and play chess while downing strong cappuccino and hearty inexpensive meals.

The cornerstone of the women-owned and -run **④** businesses in the neighborhood is the **Women's Building of the Bay Area** (3543 18th St., tel. 415/431–1180), which for more than a dozen years has held workshops and conferences of particu-

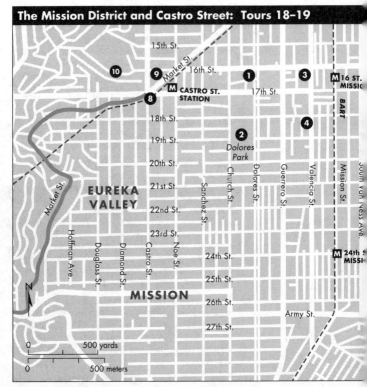

The Mission District and Castro Street: Tours 18–19

Balmy Alley, **6**

Castro
Theater, **8**

Dolores Park, **2**

Galeria de la
Raza, **5**

Josephine D.
Randall Junior
Museum, **10**

Mission
Dolores, **1**

The Names
Project, **9**

Precita Eyes and
Ears Arts
Center, **7**

Roxie Cinema, **3**

Women's
Building of the
Bay Area, **4**

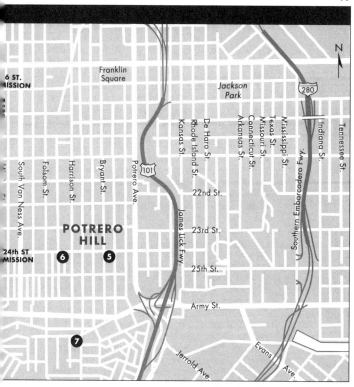

N

6 ST.
MISSION

Franklin
Square

Jackson
Park

280

Tennessee St.

Indiana St.

Southern Embarcadero Fwy.

Mississippi St.

Texas St.

Missouri St.

Connecticut St.

Arkansas St.

De Haro St.

Rhode Island St.

Kansas St.

101

Potrero Ave.

Bryant St.

Harrison St.

Folsom St.

South Van Ness Ave.

22nd St.

23rd St.

25th St.

Army St.

James Lick Fwy.

**POTRERO
HILL**

6

5

24th ST
MISSION

7

Jerrold Ave.

Evans Ave.

lar interest to women. It houses offices for many
social and political organizations and sponsors
talks and readings by such noted writers as Al-
ice Walker and Angela Davis. Bulletin boards
announce many women-oriented events in the
Bay Area.

Time Out You can eat better for less money in the Mission
District than anywhere else in the city. Stop in
at one of the *taquerias* (taco parlors), fast-food
eateries where the meals are nutritious and
very, very inexpensive. The staples are tacos
and burritos—but they are unlike those served
at Americanized fast-food places. At **La Cumbre**
(515 Valencia St., tel. 415/863–8205) and **El Toro**
(17th and Valencia Sts., tel. 415/431–3351), two
of the neighborhood's most popular taquerias,
the tacos are made with double-corn tortillas
piled high with a choice of meat and beans. And
the burritos are large, rolled-flour tortillas
stuffed with meat, rice, and beans. La Cumbre
is also well known for its *carne asada* (charcoal-
grilled steak); El Toro for its chicken simmered
in green chili sauce, and *carnitas* (crisp strips of
roast pork).

Colorful, crammed, noisy Mission Street may
represent the commercial artery of the Mission
District, but 24th Street is its heart. Here the
area takes on the flavor of another country, with
small open-air groceries selling huge Mexican
papayas and plantains, tiny restaurants serving
sopa de mariscos (fish soup), and an abundance
of religious shops and Latin bakeries. The feeling is more rural than on Mission Street and cer-
tainly less Anglo.

❺ **Galeria de la Raza,** at the east end of the street,
is an important showcase for Hispanic art. It
shows local and international artists, sometimes
mounting events in conjunction with the Mexican Museum at Fort Mason. *2855 24th St., tel.
415/826–8009. Open Tues.–Sat. noon–6.*

Next door to the Gallery is Studio 24 Galeria
Shop, which sells folklore handicrafts from Latin America. The studio specializes in figurines
from *Dia de los Muertos*, the Latin American
Halloween. The polychrome plaster skeletons—
posed as if singing, dancing, or working—rep-

resent deceased family members come back for a
visit, doing the kinds of things they did in life.
The clay groupings can be quite elaborate, using
such settings as cars, couches, and kitchens.
The aim is to make death more familiar and less
threatening; don't be surprised to see a skeleton
calmly doing her ironing. Also look for the mar-
velously detailed Peruvian tapestries called
arpedas, which also highlight daily life. *2857
24th St., tel. 415/826-8009. Open Tues. Sat.
noon-6.*

Art in the Mission District is not confined in-
doors. Keeping alive the tradition of the great
muralist Diego Rivera, community artists have
transformed the walls of their neighborhood
❻ with paintings. In small **Balmy Alley** (between
Treat and Harrison Sts. just off 24th St.), paint
changes a funky side street into a dramatic aisle
of color and purpose. The murals up and down
the alley were begun in 1973 by a group of local
children and continued by an affiliation of several dozen artists and community workers to pro-
❼ mote peace in Central America. The **Precita
Eyes and Ears Arts Center** gives guided walks of
the Mission District's murals. The tour starts
with a half-hour slide presentation, and the
walk takes about an hour, visiting over 40 murals in the area. *348 Precita Ave., tel. 415/285-
2287. Tours every Sat. at 1:30 PM. $3 adults, $1
students under 18. Walks can also be arranged
by appointment for groups of 10 or more.*

Bakeries, or *panaderias*, are an essential stop
on 24th Street. Don't expect light, buttery,
flaky creations; Latin American pastries are
strictly down-to-earth—but delicious. Try the
Salvadoran specialty, *quesadillas*, which have
cheese ground in with the flour and taste like
sweet corn muffins; or *cemitas*, cake squares
filled with pineapple. You take what looks good,
with tongs and a tray provided at the counter.
La Victoria (2937 24th St.) and **Dominguez** (2951
24th St.) on competing sides of the street are
two of the best.

The **St. Francis Fountain and Candy Store** (2801
24th St.) is a genuine soda fountain and ice-
cream parlor that makes its own confections. An

anomaly in the neighborhood, it looks like something from a Norman Rockwell painting.

Time Out Spanish, Latin American, and Caribbean *tapas* (appetizers) bars are all the rage in the Mission these days. The leader of the pack is **Esperpento,** where you can mix and match mild to spicy specialties to create a meal. The chicken croquettes are crisp outside, creamy inside, and not to be missed. Other favorites include spicy potatoes, grilled squid, and, for the more adventurous, blood sausage. Make reservations for dinner, the wait can be up to an hour. *3295 22nd St., tel. 415/282–8867. Open weekdays 11–3 and 5–10, Sat. 11–3 and 5–10:30. Closed Sun.*

The Mission District plays fiesta for two important occasions. There is a weekend of festivities around the *cinco de Mayo* (5th of May) holiday, but the neighborhood really erupts into celebration on a sunny weekend in late spring called *carnaval*. This Rio-like three-day extravaganza gets larger each year. Recent festivities closed Harrison Street between 16th and 20th streets, with four stages for live music and dancers, as well as crafts and food booths. A Grand Carnaval Parade along 24th Street caps the celebration.

Tour 19: Castro Street

Starting during the early 1970s, the neighborhood around Castro Street became known for one of the most remarkable urban migrations in American history: the mass arrival of gay men and women in San Francisco, from all over the United States. What had been for decades a sunny, sedate, middle-class neighborhood of mostly Irish and Scandinavian families became a new colony that was either a gay ghetto or, as many thought, Gay Mecca.

Historians are still trying to discover what brought an estimated 100,000 to 250,000 gays and lesbians into the San Francisco area. Some point to the libertine tradition rooted in Barbary Coast piracy, prostitution, and gambling. Others note that as a huge military embarkation point during World War II, the city was occupied by tens of thousands of mostly single men.

Whatever the cause, San Francisco became the city of choice for lesbians and gay men, and Castro Street, nestled at the base of Twin Peaks and just over Buena Vista hill from Haight Street, became its social, cultural, and political center.

From Powell Street, take the Muni Metro (trains K, L, or M) direct to the Castro Street station. You will come out into **Harvey Milk Plaza,** named for the man who electrified the city in 1977 by being voted onto the metropolitan board of supervisors as an openly gay candidate. The proprietor of a Castro Street camera store, Harvey Milk proved that the gay community of San Francisco was a political as well as a social force. His high visibility accompanied demands by homosexuals for thorough inclusion in the city's life—its power structures, not just its disco parties. San Francisco has responded with a tolerance found nowhere else in the United States: Gay people sit as municipal judges, police commissioners, and arts administrators.

Two events, though, have changed the tenor of the community. On November 27, 1978, barely a year after being elected, Harvey Milk and the liberal mayor George Moscone were assassinated by a disturbed member of the board of supervisors, Dan White. A few years later gay men began to awaken to a new terror: AIDS. The gay community has responded to this tragedy with courage and generosity. The city itself serves as a model for civic intervention and support during a health crisis. The Castro has become less flamboyant and a little more sober in the wake of the crisis; now it's more of a mixed neighborhood, and more relaxed. It is still, however, the center of gay life. Gay bars abound, and gay-oriented boutiques line Castro, 18th, and Market streets.

Across the street from Harvey Milk Plaza is the great neon neighborhood landmark, the **Castro Theater** marquee. Erected in 1922, the theater is the grandest of San Francisco's few remaining movie palaces. Its elaborate Spanish Baroque interior is well preserved, and a new pipe organ plays nightly, ending with a traditional chorus of the Jeanette McDonald standard, "San Francisco." The 1,500-capacity crowd can be enthusiastic and vocal, talking back to the screen as loudly as it talks to them. The Castro Theatre is the showcase for many community events, in particular the annual Gay/Lesbian Film Festival held each June.

Castro Street boasts numerous men's clothing stores. **All American Boy** (463 Castro St.) is the standard-bearer and setter for casual wear, especially the neighborhood uniform: jeans and T-shirts. Across the street, younger shoppers prefer the hip fashions (aka "ACT-Up chic") served up at **Rolo** (450 Castro St.). One block away, **Citizen** (536 Castro St.) counters with a more colorful selection of designer-inspired clothing.

True to its playful name, **Does Your Mother Know** (4079 18th St.) is a card store like no other, offering specialized greetings to entertain—and shock. Be prepared; this may be the premier X-rated card shop in the country. But some cards are just plain funny, with a stellar series featuring a local drag queen, the late Doris Fish, a mistress of many disguises.

A Different Light (489 Castro St.) features books by, for, and about lesbians and gay men. The store has become the unofficial Castro community center—residents regularly phone for nonbook info and a rack in the front is chock full of fliers for local events. Book-signings and poetry readings occur several times each week.

Time Out There are several renowned gay chefs in San Francisco. Unfortunately, none of them work in the Castro, where a half-dozen greasy spoons do surprisingly well. Festive **Pozole,** which serves burritos, quesadillas, and other Mexican and Latin American specialties, is a welcome recent addition to the neighborhood. *2337 Market St., tel. 415/626-2666. Open Mon.–Thurs. 4–11, Fri.–Sun. noon–midnight.*

---

❾ Down Market Street **The Names Project** (2362 Market St.) has its public workshop. A gigantic quilt made of more than 10,000 hand-sewn and -decorated panels has been pieced together by loved ones to serve as a memorial to those who have died of AIDS. People come from all over the country to work in this storefront as a labor of love and grief; others have sent panels here by mail. New additions to the quilt are always on display. The site serves as a dignified in-progress tribute to a community's struggle and compassionate involvement. **Under One Roof** (tel. 415/252–9430; open Sun.–Fri. 11–7, Sat. 10–8) is a store at the same address that sells T-shirts, posters, and other merchandise to raise funds for various AIDS organizations.

Just northwest of Castro and Market streets, an outcropping of rock provides one of the best viewing areas in the city. Walk north up Castro Street two blocks to 16th Street and turn left. This is a steep climb, and it gets steeper and a little more rugged, but it's worth the effort. Turn right at Flint Street; the hill to your left is variously known as Red Rock, Museum Hill, and, correctly, Corona Heights. Start climbing up the path by the tennis courts along the spine of the hill; the view downtown is increasingly superb. You don't have to go very high up to have all of northeast San Francisco and the bay before you. In spring you'll be surrounded by California wildflowers, but whenever you climb to the ragged rocks at the top, be sure to carry a jacket with you: The wind loves this spot.

❿ At the base of Corona Heights is the **Josephine D. Randall Junior Museum.** Geared toward children by the Recreation and Parks Department, the museum nevertheless has a variety of workshops and events for both young people and their parents. It includes a Mineral Hall, Animal Room, library, and an excellent woodworking studio. *199 Museum Way, tel. 415/554–9600. The museum is open Tues.–Sat. 10–5 and at night for workshops. The Animal Room is open 10:30–1 and 2–5.*

The Castro neighborhood is allied to three events that are true community holidays. In late September or early October, when San Francisco weather is at its warmest, the annual Castro Street Fair takes over several blocks of Castro and Market streets. Huge stages are erected for live music and comedy, alongside booths selling food and baubles. The weather inevitably brings off the men's shirts, and the Castro relives for a moment the permissive spirit of the 1970s. Each

Halloween thousands of revelers (though most are just onlookers) converge on Castro Street from all over the city to watch the perpetual masquerade. Drag queens of all shapes and sizes intentionally reduce the crowd to laughter; the spirit is high and friendly, San Francisco's version of Mardi Gras.

More political is the annual Lesbian/Gay Pride Celebration and Parade, by far the city's largest annual event. On the last Sunday in June 250,000 to 500,000 men and women march to the Civic Center to commemorate the birth of the modern gay-rights movement. This is no longer a parochial march; major political figures participate, and it regularly provides the gay community with its most powerful public statement.

Tour 20: Haight-Ashbury

East of Golden Gate Park is the neighborhood known as "the Haight." Once home to large, middle-class families of European immigrants, the Haight began to change during the late 1950s and early 1960s. Families were fleeing to the suburbs; the big old Victorians were deteriorating or being chopped up into cheap housing. Young people found the neighborhood an affordable and exciting community in which to live according to new precepts.

The peak of the Haight as a youth scene came in 1966. It had become the home of many rock bands. The Grateful Dead moved into a big Victorian at 710 Ashbury Street, just a block off Haight Street. Jefferson Airplane had their grand mansion at 2400 Fulton Street. By 1967, 200,000 young people with flowers in their hair were heading for the Haight. The peace and civil rights movements had made "freedom" their generation's password.

Sharing the late-1980s fascination with things of the 1960s, many visitors to San Francisco want to see the setting of the "Summer of Love." Back in 1967, Gray Lines instituted their "Hippie-Hop," advertising it as "the only foreign tour within the continental limits of the United States," piloted by a driver "especially trained in the sociological significance of the Haight." Today's explorers can walk from Union Square

to Market Street and hop aboard Muni's No. 7
Haight.

Haight Street has once again emerged as the
center of youth culture in San Francisco, though
this time it is an amalgam of punkers, neo-hippies, and suburbanites out to spend their cash.
The street has become the city's prime shopping
district for "vintage" merchandise.

While it increases the incidence of panhandlers
and the visibility of the homeless, Golden Gate
Park also provides the Haight with unique opportunities for recreation and entertainment.
You can rent roller skates at **Skates on Haight**
(1818 Haight St.) and roll through the park (it's
partially closed to traffic for skaters on Sundays); or you can take the more genteel route
and rent bicycles at several stops along Stanyan
Street, right by the park's entrance.

The Haight's famous political spirit (it was the
first neighborhood in the United States to lead a
freeway revolt, and it continues to feature regular boycotts against chain stores said to ruin the
street's local character) exists alongside some of
the finest Victorian-lined streets in the city;
more than 1,000 such houses occupy the Panhan-
dle and Ashbury Heights streets.

Great city views can be had from **Buena Vista
Park** at Haight and Lyon streets. One of San
Francisco's most attractive bed-and-breakfast
inns is the **Spreckels Mansion** at 737 Buena Vista
West, several blocks south of Haight Street. The
house was built for sugar baron Richard
Spreckels in 1887, and later tenants included
Jack London and Ambrose Bierce.

What to See and Do with Children

The attractions described in the exploring sec-
tions, above, offer a great deal of entertainment
for children as well as their families. We suggest, for example, visiting the ships at the **Hyde
Street Pier** and spending some time at **Pier 39,**
where there is a double-decker Venetian carousel. (*See* Tour 14: The Northern Waterfront,
above.)

Children will find much to amuse themselves
with at **Golden Gate Park,** from the old-fash-

ioned conservatory to the expansive lawns and trails. There is another vintage carousel (1912) at the children's playground. The **Steinhart Aquarium** at the California Academy of Sciences has a "Touching Tide Pool," from which docents will pull starfish and hermit crabs for children or adults to feel. The **Japanese Tea Garden,** although crowded, is well worth exploring; climbing over the high, humpbacked bridges is like moving the neighborhood playground toys into an exotic new (or old) world.

It is also possible to walk across the **Golden Gate Bridge.** The view is thrilling and the wind invigorating, if the children (and adults) are not overwhelmed by the height of the bridge and the nearby automobile traffic. (*See* Tour 15: The Marina and the Presidio, *above.*)

Many children may enjoy walking along crowded **Grant Avenue** and browsing in the many souvenir shops. Unfortunately, nothing— not even straw finger wrestlers, wooden contraptions to make coins "disappear," shells that open in water to release tissue paper flowers, and other true junk—is as cheap as it once was. (*See* Tour 6: Chinatown, *above.*)

The **San Francisco Zoo,** with a children's zoo, playground, and carousel, is not far from Ocean Beach. The weather and the currents do not allow swimming, but it's a good place for walking and playing in the surf. (*See* Tour 17: Lincoln Park and the Western Shoreline, *above.*)

The **Exploratorium** at the Palace of Fine Arts is a preeminent children's museum and is very highly recommended. (*See* Tour 15: The Marina and the Presidio, *above.*)

3   Shopping

By Sheila Gadsden

San Franciscan Sheila Gadsden has worked as an editor and writer for Woman's Day, Motorland, Travel & Leisure, San Francisco, *and many others.*

San Francisco is a shopper's dream—major department stores, fine fashion, discount outlets, art galleries, and crafts stores are among the many offerings. Most accept at least Visa and MasterCard charge cards, and many also accept American Express, and Diner's Club. A very few accept cash only. Ask about traveler's checks; policies vary. The *San Francisco Chronicle* and *Examiner* advertise sales; for smaller innovative shops, check the San Francisco *Bay Guardian*. Store hours are slightly different everywhere, but a generally trusted rule is to shop between 10 AM and 5 or 6 PM Monday–Wednesday, Friday, and Saturday; between 10 AM and 8 or 9 PM on Thursday; and from noon until 5 PM on Sunday. Stores on and around Fisherman's Wharf often have longer summer hours.

Major Shopping Districts

Fisherman's Wharf San Francisco's Fisherman's Wharf is host to a number of shopping and sightseeing attractions: **Pier 39, the Anchorage, Ghirardelli Square,** and **The Cannery.** Each offers shops, restaurants, and a festive atmosphere as well as such outdoor entertainment as musicians, mimes, and magicians. Pier 39 includes an amusement area and a double-decked Venetian carousel. One attraction shared by all the centers is the view of the bay and the proximity of the cable car lines, which can take shoppers directly to Union Square.

Union Square Serious shoppers will find the entire Union Square area richly rewarding. Bordering the square itself are leading department and specialty stores. **I. Magnin & Co.,** on the south side of Union Square at Stockton Street, is noted for its designer fashions, magnificent fur salon, and precious jewelry salon. Just across Stockton Street is the checker-board-faced **Neiman Marcus,** opened in 1982. Philip Johnson's controversial design replaced an old San Francisco favorite, the City of Paris; all that remains is the great glass dome. **Macy's,** with entrances on Geary, Stockton, and O'Farrell streets, has huge selections of clothing, plus extensive furniture and household accessories departments. The men's department—one of the world's largest—occupies its own building across Stockton Street. Opposite is the new **FAO Schwarz** children's store, with its extravagant assortment of life-size stuffed animals, animated displays, and steep prices. **Saks Fifth Avenue,** at the northwest corner of the square at Post and Powell streets, still caters to the upscale shopper. Nearby are the pricey international boutiques of Hermes of Paris, Gucci, Celine of Paris, Alfred Dunhill, Louis Vuitton, and Cartier.

Across from the cable car turntable at Powell and Market streets is the **San Francisco Shopping Centre,** with the fashionable **Nordstrom's** department store and more than 35 other shops. And underneath a glass dome at Post and Kearny streets is **Crocker Galleria,** a complex of 50 shops and restaurants topped by two rooftop parks.

Embarcadero Center Five modern towers of shops, restaurants, and offices plus the Hyatt Regency Hotel make up the downtown Embarcadero Center at the end of Market Street. Like most malls, the center is a little sterile and falls short in the character department. What it lacks in charm, however, it makes up for in sheer quantity. The center's 175 stores and services include such nationally known stores as **The Limited, B. Dalton Bookseller,** and **Ann Taylor,** as well as more local or West Coast-based businesses such as the **Nature Company, Filian's European Clothing,** and **Lotus Designer Earrings.** Each tower occupies one block, and parking garages are available.

Jackson Square Jackson Square is where a dozen or so of San Francisco's finest retail antiques dealers are located. If your passion is 19th-century English furniture, for example, there's a good chance that something here will suit. Knowledgeable store owners and staffs can direct you to other places in the city for your special interests. The shops are along Jackson Street in the Financial District, so a visit there will put you very close to the Embarcadero Center and Chinatown.

Chinatown The intersection of Grant Avenue and Bush Street marks "the Gateway" to Chinatown; here shoppers and tourists are introduced to 24 blocks of shops, restaurants, markets, and tem-

Downtown San Francisco Shopping

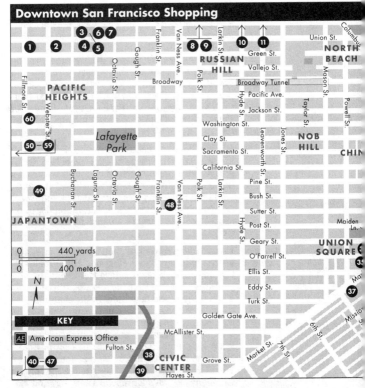

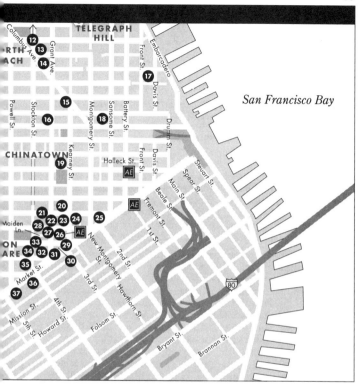

Krazy Kaps, **12**
Ma-Shi'-Ko
Folk Craft, **49**
Macy's, **34**
Nordstrom, **37**
North Beach
Leather, **33**
The North
Face, **23**
Old and New
Estates, **1**
Origins, **45**

Paris 1925, **5**
Patagonia, **10**
Patronik
Designs, **4**
Peluche, **54**
Revival of the
Fittest, **46**
Santa Fe, **59**
Scheuer
Linen, **31**
The Sharper
Image, **17, 25**

Shreve &
Co., **21**
Spellbound, **44**
Sy Aal, **7**
Telegraph Hill
Antiques, **13**
Virginia
Breier, **56**
Vorpal
Gallery, **38**
Walter
McIntres, **57**

Wholesale
Jewelers
Exchange, **35**
Yankee Doodle
Dandy, **3**
Yountville, **60**
Z Gallerie, **2**

ples. There are daily "sales" on gems of all
sorts—especially jade and pearls—alongside
stalls of bok choy and gingerroot. Chinese silks
and toy trinkets are also commonplace in the
shops, as are selections of colorful pottery, baskets, and large figures of soapstone, ivory, and
jade, including *netsukes* (carved figures).

North Beach The once largely Italian enclave of North Beach
gets smaller each year as Chinatown spreads
northward. It has been called the city's answer
to New York City's Greenwich Village, although
it's much smaller. Many of the businesses here
tend to be small clothing stores, antiques shops,
or such eccentric specialty shops as **Quantity
Postcard** (1441 Grant Ave., tel. 415/986–8866),
which has an inventory of 15,000 different
postcards. If you get tired of poking around in
the bookstores, a number of cafés dot the streets
and there are lots of Italian restaurants.

The Marina Chestnut Street caters to the shopping needs of
District Marina District residents. It offers more of a
neighborhood feeling than do other well-
touristed shopping areas. Banks and well-
known stores, including **Waldenbooks, The Gap,**
and **Lucca Delicatessen Goods,** are interspersed
with such unique gift shops as the **Red Rose
Gallerie,** which specializes in "tools for personal
growth," including body scents, exotic clothing,
and audiotapes for rejuvenating the mind.
Shops start at Fillmore Street and end at
Broderick Street.

Union Street Out-of-towners sometimes confuse Union
Street—a popular stretch of shops and restaurants five blocks south of the Golden Gate National Recreation Area—with downtown's
Union Square (*see above*). Nestled at the foot of
a hill between the neighborhoods of Pacific
Heights and Cow Hollow, Union Street shines
with contemporary fashion and custom jewelry.
Union Street's feel is largely new and upscale,
although there are a few antiques shops and
some long-term storekeepers. Here are some local favorites: The wild yet elegant contemporary art furniture at **Arte Forma** (1775 Union
St.) includes multicolored leather sofas and
eerie rice-paper lamps by Noguchi. **Images of
the North** (1782 Union St.) specializes in superb

Inuit art from Alaska and Canada. **Laura Ashley**
(1827 Union St.) brings a touch of Edwardian elegance to the street. Down the way, the epoch
switches to Victorian, where naughty-but-nice
romantic lingerie lies behind the quaint doors of
Victoria's Secret (2245 Union St.) If you like
country furnishings, be sure to view the pre-
1935 American quilt collection at **Yankee Doodle
Dandy** (1974 Union St.) Delight a youngster
with a charming stuffed animal made of vintage
quilt bits.

Pacific   When Pacific Heights residents look for practi-
Heights   cal services, they look toward Fillmore and Sacramento streets. Both streets feel more like
neighborhood streets than upscale shopping areas, and that is exactly their appeal to tourists
and natives—easygoing and personal with good
bookstores, fine clothing shops, gift shops,
thrift stores, and furniture and art galleries.
Sue Fisher King Company (3067 Sacramento St.)
is an eclectic collection of home accessories, and
Yountville (2416 Fillmore St.) has lovely
children's clothing from local and European designers. The Fillmore Street shopping area
runs from Post Street to Pacific Avenue. Most
shops on the western end of Sacramento Street
are between Lyon and Maple streets.

Japantown   Unlike Chinatown, North Beach, or the Mission, the 5-acre **Japan Center** (between Laguna
and Fillmore Sts., and between Geary and Post
Sts.) is contained under one roof. It is actually a
mall of stores filled with antique kimonos, beautiful tansu chests, and both new and old porcelains. The center always feels a little empty, but
the good shops here are well worth a visit. Here
are some of the more interesting places to
browse: **Soko Hardware** (1698 Post St.), which
has been run by the Ashizawa merchant family
since 1925, specializes in beautifully crafted
Japanese tools for gardening and carpentry.
They also have those long-sleeved, back-fasten-
ing Japanese aprons. **Nichi Bei Bussan** (1715 Buchanan St.) has a collector's choice of quilts
covered with fabulous Japanese designs. Prices
start at about $75. Charming baby's **chan-chan-
ko** (tiny printed Japanese-style vests) and re-
frigerator-door magnets in sushi motifs are popular gifts. **Kinokuniya,** on the second floor of the

center's western-most Kinokuniya Building, may have the finest selection of English-language books on Japanese subjects in the United States. There are books on food, *ikebana* (the art of flower arranging), Japanese philosophy, religion, literature, and art, plus a large selection of elegant calendars. **Asakichi,** on the first floor of the Kinokuniya Building, specializes in antique blue-and-white Imari porcelains and handsome *tansu* (chests). Collector's of art-to-wear search for antique hand-painted, silk-embroidered kimonos at **Shige Antiques,** on the bridge to the Kintetsu Building. The Arita porcelains, silk calligraphy scrolls, tea-ceremony utensils, and treasured lacquerware boxes at this store will dazzle aficionados. The shops in the **Tamasak Plaza Building** are a paradise for souvenir shoppers. Colorful flying-fish kites and delicate floral-patterned cocktail napkins are popular choices.

The Haight Haight Street is always an attraction for visitors, if only to see the sign at Haight and Ashbury streets—the geographic center of flower power during the 1960s. These days, instead of tie-dye shirts you'll find good-quality vintage clothing, funky jewelry, art from Mexico, and reproductions of Art Deco accessories. (*see* Vintage Fashion and Vintage Furniture and Accessories, *below*). The street also boasts several used-book stores and some of the best used-record stores in the city: **Recycled Records** (1377 Haight St.), **Reckless Records** (1401 Haight St.), and **Rough Trade** (1529 Haight St.) focus on classic rock-and-roll, obscure independent labels, and hard-to-find imports.

Civic Center The shops and galleries that have sprung up around the Civic Center reflect the cultural offerings of Davies Symphony Hall, Herbst Auditorium, the Opera House, and the Museum of Modern Art. The area is a little sparse compared with other tightly packed shopping streets in the city, but it is well worth a visit. The **San Francisco Opera Shop** (199 Grove St., tel. 415/565–6414), across Van Ness Avenue from Davies Hall, is packed with recordings, books, posters, and gift items associated with the performing arts. The tree-lined block of Hayes Street between Gough and Franklin streets includes art galleries, crafts shops, and pleasant cafés. This area includes Hayes and Grove streets from Polk Street and extends just past Octavia Street.

South of Market In keeping with SoMa's tradition of being the underside of the city, it now offers you the underside of shopping: discount outlets. Dozens, most of them open seven days a week, have sprung along the streets and alleyways bordered by 2nd, Twonsend, Howard and 9th streets. A good place to start is across from the Cartoon Art Museum at the **660 Factory Outlets Center** (660 Third St., tel. 415/227–0464; open Mon.–Sat. 10–5:30, Sun. noon–5.), 22 shops that offer everything from designer fashions to Icelandic sweaters. The chief attraction at the Yerba Buena Square at Fifth and Howard is the **Burlington** outlet (tel. 415/495–7234; open Mon.–Sat. 9:30 AM–8 PM, Sun. 11–6), but you'll find bargains on toys, shoes, and other items as well. The city's first mega-outlet, **Esprit** (499 Illinois Ave., tel. 415/957–2550; open weekdays 10–8, Sat. 10–7, Sun. 11–5), is in the Portrero District less than a mile south of the 660 Factory Outlet. The Esprit shop is no longer as jammed as it was a few years ago, but good buys are still to be had.

Department Stores

Emporium (835 Market St., tel. 415/764–2222). This full-service department store carries a complete line of clothing and home furnishings. The prices are reasonable compared with those you'll find at many downtown department stores.

Macy's (Stockton and O'Farrell Sts., tel. 415/397–3333). Designer fashions, an extensive array of shoes, household wares, furniture, food, and even a post office and foreign currency exchange.

Nordstrom (865 Market St., tel. 415/243–8500). This large downtown store is known for providing excellent service to customers. The building's stunning interior design features spiral escalators circling a four-story atrium. Designer fashions, shoes, accessories, and cosmetics are specialties.

Three other large stores that offer high-quality merchandise are **I. Magnin, Neiman Marcus,** and **Saks Fifth Avenue** (all are on Union Square).

Specialty Stores

Antique Furniture **Origins** (637 Townsend St., tel. 415/252–7089). This large Asian antique store—part of the Baker Hamilton Square complex in the South of Market area—imports unusual collector's items, Chinese furniture, porcelain, silk, and jade. It's not unheard of to find a piece up to 400 years old here. The complex houses more than a dozen other antique furniture shops, which, among them, cover quite a few different periods and styles, ranging from Thai to Art Deco to 19th-century French and English pieces.

Fumiki (2001 Union St., tel. 415/922–0573). This store offers a fine selection of Asian arts, including antiques, art, fine jewelry, Chinese silk paintings, and Korean and Japanese furniture. Two specialties here are *obis* (sashes worn with kimonos) and antique Japanese baskets. Other good sources for Japanese antiques are **Genji** and **Asakichi,** both in Japan Center.

Glen Smith Galleries (2021 Fillmore St., tel. 415/931–3081). The specialties here are 18th- and 19th-century furniture, porcelain, glass, and decorative arts. The gallery is open Tuesday–Saturday 10–5 or by appointment; it is closed noon–1 PM.

Hunt Antiques (478 Jackson St., tel. 415/989–9531). Fine 17th- to 19th-century period English furniture as well as porcelains, Staffordshire pottery, prints, clocks, and paintings in a gracious country-house setting can be found here. This is only one of a dozen or so shops in the Jackson Square area. Others such as **Foster-Gwin Antiques, Carpets of the Inner Circle,** and the **Antiques Gallery,** are also fine bets.

Telegraph Hill Antiques (580 Union St., tel. 415/982–7055). A very mixed but fine selection is available in this little North Beach shop: fine china and porcelain, crystal, cut glass, Oriental objects, Victoriana, bronzes, and paintings. Open Monday–Saturday to 5:30 or by appointment.

Walker McIntyre (3419 Sacramento St., tel. 415/563–8024). This shop specializes in pieces from the Georgian period, but it also offers 19th-century Japanese Imari cloisonné, lamps custom-made from antique vases, and Oriental rugs. Other very fine antiques stores on this street include **Hawley Bragg, Robert Hering,** and **Claire Thomson.**

Antique Jewelry **J. M. Lang** (323 Sutter St., tel. 415/982–2213). This is another good source for both jewelry and small antique objects, particularly fine glass, amber, and silver.
Old and New Estates (2181-A Union St., tel. 415/346–7525). This shop offers both antique and modern jewelry, crystal, and silver. It is generally open on weekdays and Saturdays 11–6, but the hours vary, so it's best to call first.
Paris 1925 (1954 Union St., tel. 415/567–1925) specializes in estate jewelry and vintage watches.

Art Galleries There are dozens of art galleries scattered throughout the city. Most surround downtown Union Square, although in recent years some of the interest has shifted to the newly thriving Hayes Valley area near the Civic Center and South of Market. Pick up a copy of the free *San Francisco Arts Monthly* at TIX Bay Area for listings of other galleries in the area and elsewhere in the city.

Harcourts Gallery (460 Bush St., tel. 415/421–3428). One of the city's best-known galleries, Harcourts exhibits paintings, sculpture, and graphics by 19th- and 20th-century artists, including Picasso, Chagall, Renoir, and Miró, as well as works by contemporary artists such as Robert Rauschenberg, Sylvia Glass, and Roland Petersen. Open Tuesday–Saturday.
Vorpal Gallery (393 Grove St., tel. 415/397–9200). A premier gallery that focuses on postmodern painting, drawing, and sculpture, Vorpal's also has an excellent collection of graphic arts.

Books **City Lights** (261 Columbus Ave., tel. 415/362–8193). The city's most famous bookstore—and possibly the most comfortable bookstore for browsing—this was a major center for poetry readings during the 1960s. City Lights publishes books as well. The store is particularly well stocked in poetry, contemporary literature and music, and translations of third-world literature. There is also an interesting selection of books on nature, the outdoors, and travel. Open daily 10 AM–midnight.

Kinokuniya Bookstores (1581 Webster St., tel. 415/567–7625). This Japan Center store offers all sorts of books and periodicals in Japanese and English, but a major attraction is the collection of beautifully produced graphics and art books. Closed first Tuesday of every month.

Other excellent bookstores in the city include **Solar Light Books** (general needs), **The Sierra Club Bookstore** (California and the West), and **William Stout Architectural Books** (for interiors, exteriors, graphics, and landscape design).

Fabrics **Edward's Unusual Fabrics** (80 Geary St., tel. 415/397–5625). This store offers another fine selection of fabrics, especially good silks.

Far East Fashion (953 Grant Ave., tel. 415/362–8171 or 362–0986). This store has one of Chinatown's better selections of Chinese embossed silks and lace.

Fine Gifts and Specialty Items **Biordi** (412 Columbus Ave., tel. 415/392–8096). In the heart of North Beach, this small colorful store sells Majolica dinnerware and other imported Italian handicrafts and ceramics.

Other good specialty stores are **Yone** in North Beach (for beads), the **Sharper Image** downtown (gadgets), and **Waterford Wedgwood** on Union Square (crystal and china).

Clothing for Children **Dottie Doolittle** (3680 Sacramento St., tel. 415/563–3244). This store offers domestic and imported clothing sized from infant to 14 years, as well as baby furniture.

Yountville (2416 Fillmore St., tel. 415/922–5050). California and European designs are the draw here, from infant to 8 years.

Clothing for Men and Women **Apacci Paris** (50 Grant Ave., tel. 415/982–7222). This exclusive store sells a collection of menswear from Italy, France, and Switzerland. It is known for its unique ties.

Brava Strada (3247 Sacramento St., tel. 415/567–5757). Featured here are designer knitwear and accessories; Italian and other European leather goods; and one-of-a-kind jewelry from American and European artists. Also on

Sacramento Street is **Button Down,** carrying "updated traditional" clothing and accessories.

Eileen West (33 Grant Ave., tel. 415/982–2275). San Francisco designer Eileen West displays her lovely dresses, sleepwear, lingerie, linens, and more in this cozy boutique.

Jeanne Marc (262 Sutter St., tel. 415/362–1121). This boutique sells sportswear and more formal clothes in the striking prints that have become the hallmark of this San Francisco designer.

Justine (3263 Sacramento St., tel. 415/921–8548). Women's clothes by French designers Dorothee Bis, George Rech, and Ventilo are the draw here, as well as shoes by Charles Kammer.

Kilkenny Shop (Ghirardelli Sq., 900 N. Point St., tel. 415/771–8984). Irish handwoven shawls, and throws, dresses, tweed hats, and other accessories are sold here.

Krazy Kaps (Pier 39, tel. 415/296–8930). Here you'll find silly hats as well as top hats, Stetsons, and Greek fishermen's caps—a good assortment for personal use and gift giving.

Peluche (3366 Sacramento St., tel. 415/346–6361). This shop specializes in one-of-a-kind, hand-knit sweaters, mostly from Italy, and European fashions for women.

Sy Aal (1864 Union St., tel. 415/929–1864). Offering "men's fashion with a woman's point of view," Sy Aal carries a full line of fine clothing, including hand-knits, and specializes in ties.

Other good places for women's clothing stores are Union Square; Crocker Galleria, which has such famously known shops as **Casual Corner;** and the Embarcadero Center, whose selection includes **Ann Taylor, The Limited,** and **Banana Republic.**

Handicrafts and Folk Art

Cottonwood (3461 Sacramento St., tel. 415/346–6020). Fine handcrafted home furnishings and decorative objects, including flatware, dinnerware, leather boxes, sculpture, and baskets abound in this store.

F. Dorian (388 Hayes St., tel. 415/861–3191). Cards, jewelry, and other crafts from Mexico, Japan, Italy, Peru, Indonesia, Philippines, and Sri Lanka as well as items from local craftspeople are the specialties here.

Folk Art International Gallery (Ghirardelli Sq., 900 N. Point St., tel. 415/441–6100). This gallery features an extensive contemporary folk-art collection from Mexico, China, Ecuador, France, Sri Lanka, Peru, Haiti, and other countries—masks, boxes, sculpture, baskets, toys, and textiles. The adjoining gallery, **Xanadu** (tel. 415/441–5211), offers artifacts and tribal art from Asia, Africa, Oceania, and the Americas.

Japonesque (824 Montgomery St., tel. 415/398–8577). Here you'll find handcrafted wooden boxes, sculpture, paintings, and handmade glass from Japan and the United States.

Ma-Shi'-Ko Folk Craft (1581 Webster St., Japan Center, tel. 415/346–0748). This store carries handcrafted pottery from Japan, including Mashiko, the style that has been in production longer than any other. There are also masks and other handcrafted goods, all from Japan.

Santa Fe (3571 Sacramento St., tel. 415/346–0180). This is where you'll find old Navajo rugs, ranch furniture, old silver and turquoise jewelry, Indian pots and baskets, and cowboy relics.

Virginia Breier (3091 Sacramento St., tel. 415/929–7173). A colorful gallery of contemporary and ethnic crafts from Mexico, Indonesia, Korea, Japan, Brazil, and the United States, especially the West Coast; includes decorative and functional items, antiques.

Yankee Doodle Dandy (1974 Union St., tel. 415/346–0346). A large selection of American antique quilts, carvings, handmade stuffed animals, woven throws.

Other shops to look at are **Oggetti** on Union Street, which carries Italian marbelized papers and gifts; **Designs in Motion** at Pier 39; **Images of the North** on Union Street; **Artifacts** on Fillmore Street; and **Xoxo** on Hayes Street.

Jewelry **Jade Empire** (832 Grant Ave., tel. 415/982–4498). One of the many fine jewelry stores in Chinatown, this one has good jade, diamonds, and other gems.

Patronik Designs (1949 Union St., tel. 415/922–9716). Innovative contemporary and custom jewelry. Other good stores on Union are **Union Street Goldsmith** and **David Clay.**

Shreve & Co. (Post St. and Grant Ave., tel. 415/421–2600). One of the city's most elegant jewelers, and the oldest retail store in San Francisco, is near Union Square.

Wholesale Jewelers Exchange (121 O'Farrell St., tel. 415/788–2365). This is a source for fine gems and finished jewelry at less than retail prices.

Leather **The Coach Store** (190 Post St., tel. 415/392–1772). A branch of the nationally known purveyor of classically designed leather goods, the inventory here includes purses, briefcases, silk scarves, and belts and wallets of all sizes, colors, and weights.

North Beach Leather (190 Geary St., tel. 415/362–8300). One of the best sources for high-quality leather garments—skirts, jackets, pants, dresses, accessories. With its sculpted walls, the store itself is a work of art. The original store is still in business at Fisherman's Wharf (1365 Columbus Ave., tel. 415/441–3208).

Linens **Claire's Antique Linens & Gifts** (3615 Sacramento St., tel. 415/776–9352). Nationally known for Victorian and Edwardian tablecloths and bedspreads. (The store is true to its name; only about 1% of the items are new.) It also sells crystal and china. Everything is available in a wide range of prices.

Scheuer Linen (318 Stockton St., tel. 415/392–2813). Luxurious linens for the bed, the bath, and the dining table abound here, including European linens and special designs.

Miscellaneous **Aerial** (The Cannery, 2801 Leavenworth St., tel. 415/474–1566). Here you'll find an eclectic mix of goods—soaps, art supplies, handcrafted leather boxes, clothes, pewter flasks, sunglasses, compasses, and lots of unusual but functional objects.

Z Gallerie (2071 Union St., tel. 415/346–9000; Stonestown Galleria, 3251 20th Ave., tel. 415/664–7891). Home furnishings in black—butterfly chairs, dinnerware, desks, chairs, lamps, and a variety of high-tech accessories—are the specialties here; also posters, both black-and-white and color. There are other stores in the San Francisco Shopping Centre on Market Street and on Haight Street.

Sporting **The North Face** (180 Post St. and 1325 Howard
Goods St. (outlet), tel. 415/626–6444). This Bay Area-based company is famous for its top-of-the-line tents, sleeping bags, backpacks, skis, and out-

door apparel, including stylish Gore-Tex jackets and pants.

Patagonia (770 Northpoint, near Fisherman's Wharf, tel. 415/771–2050). The outdoorsy set will want to check out Patagonia's signature parkas and jackets.

Toiletries **Body Time** (2072 Union St., tel. 415/922–4076). These are some of the best concoctions around for the face and body—locally produced soaps, lotions, creams, perfumes, and body oils.

Toys and **FAO Schwarz Fifth Avenue** (88 Stockton St., tel. **Gadgets** 415/394–8700). The San Francisco branch of an American tradition, this store features a little of everything, from games and stuffed toys to motorized cars and trains.

Forma (1715 Haight St., tel. 415/751–0545) is one of the most imaginative shops in the city, with items ranging from design accessories by artists to 1950s-style lava lamps and toy animals inspired by Japanese monster movies.

Kids Only (1415 Haight St., tel. 415/552–5445). A children's emporium, this store has a little bit of everything.

The Sharper Image (532 Market St., tel. 415/ 398–6472; 680 Davis St. at Broadway, tel. 415/ 445–6100). This paradise for gadget lovers features everything from five-language translators and super-shock-absorbent tennis racquets to state-of-the-art speaker systems and walkman-size computers. Also at Ghirardelli Square.

Vintage **American Rag** (1035 Van Ness Ave., tel. 415/ **Fashion** 474–5214). Stocked here is a large, department-store-like selection of men's and women's clothes from the United States and Europe, all in excellent shape. They also stock shoes and accessories such as sunglasses, hats, belts, and scarves.

Buffalo Exchange (1555 Haight St., tel. 415/ 431–7733). One of five stores in the Bay Area and in Arizona, the Haight Street store sells both new and recycled clothing and will also trade items. Also at 1800 Polk Street.

Held Over (1543 Haight St., tel. 415/864–0818). An extensive collection of clothing from the 1940s, '50s, and '60s.

Spellbound (1670 Haight St., tel. 415/863–4930). Fine fashions from decades past—including bugle-beaded dresses, silk scarves, and suits—are offered here. Some of the inventory comes from estate sales.

Vintage Furniture and Accessories

Dish.ar.ray (637 Townsend St., tel. 415/252–7008). Part of the Baker Hamilton Square complex of antique stores, this cozy shop specializes in Art Deco memorabilia and collectibles such as pottery and clocks.

Revival of the Fittest (1701 Haight St., tel. 415/751–8857). Telephones, dishes, assorted collectibles, as well as vintage and reproduction jewelry, clocks, lamps, vases, and furniture can be found here.

4 Dining

By Jacqueline Killeen

Jacqueline Killeen has been writing about San Francisco restaurants for over 25 years. She is a restaurant critic for San Francisco Focus *magazine.*

San Francisco probably has more restaurants per capita than any other city in the United States, including New York. Practically every ethnic cuisine is represented. That makes selecting some 90 restaurants to list here from the vast number available a very difficult task indeed. We have chosen several restaurants to represent each popular style of dining in various price ranges, in most cases because of the superiority of the food, but in some instances because of the view or ambience.

All listed restaurants serve dinner and are open for lunch unless otherwise specified; restaurants are not open for breakfast unless the morning meal is specifically mentioned.

Parking accommodations are mentioned only when a restaurant has made special arrangements; otherwise you're on your own. There is usually a charge for valet parking. Validated parking is not necessarily free and unlimited; often there is a nominal charge and a restriction on the length of time.

Restaurants do change their policies about hours, credit cards, and the like. It is always best to make inquiries in advance.

The most highly recommended restaurants are indicated by a star ★.

The price ranges listed below are for an average three-course meal. A significant trend among more expensive restaurants is the bar menu, which provides light snacks—hot dogs, chili, pizza, and appetizers—in the bar for a cost that is often less than $10 for two.

Category	Cost*
Very Expensive	over $45
Expensive	$30–$45
Moderate	$18–$30
Inexpensive	under $18

per person, excluding drinks, service, and 8½% sales tax

The following credit card abbreviations are
used: AE, American Express; DC, Diner's
Club; MC, MasterCard; V, Visa. Many restaurants accept cards other than those listed here,
and some will accept personal checks if you carry a major credit card.

American

Before the 1980s, it was hard to find a decent
"American" restaurant in the Bay Area. In recent years, however, the list has been growing
and become more diversified, with fare that includes barbecue, Southwestern, all-American
diner food, and that mix of Mediterranean-
Asian-Latino known as California cuisine.

Civic Center
★
Stars. This is the culinary temple of Jeremiah
Tower, the superchef who claims to have invented California cuisine. Stars is a must on every traveling gourmet's itinerary, but it's also
where many of the local movers and shakers
hang out, a popular place for post-theater dining, and open till the wee hours. The dining
room has a clublike ambience, and the food
ranges from grills to ragouts to sautées—some
daringly creative and some classical. Dinners
here are pricey, but you can eat on a budget with
a hot dog at the bar or by standing in line for a
table at the informal Star's Cafe next door. *150
Redwood Alley, tel. 415/861-7827. Reservations accepted up to 2 wks in advance, some tables reserved for walk-ins. Dress: informal.
AE, DC, MC, V. No lunch weekends. Closed
Thanksgiving, Christmas. Valet parking at
night. Expensive.*

Embarcadero
North
★
Fog City Diner. This is where the diner and graz-
ing crazes began in San Francisco, and the popularity of this spot knows no end. The long,
narrow dining room emulates a luxurious rail-
road car with dark wood paneling, huge windows, and comfortable booths. The cooking is
innovative, drawing its inspiration from regional cooking throughout the United States. The
sharable "small plates" are a fun way to go. *1300
Battery St., tel. 415/982-2000. Reservations advised. Dress: informal. DC, MC, V. Closed
Thanksgiving and Christmas. Moderate.*
MacArthur Park. Year after year San Francis-

cans acclaim this as their favorite spot for ribs, but the oakwood smoker and mesquite grill also turn out a wide variety of all-American fare, from steaks, hamburgers, and chili to seafood. Takeout is also available at this handsomely renovated pre-earthquake warehouse. *607 Front St., tel. 415/398–5700. Reservations advised. Dress: informal. AE, DC, MC, V. No lunch weekends and major holidays. Closed Thanksgiving and Christmas. Valet parking at night. Moderate.*

Financial **Cypress Club.** Fans of John Cunin have flocked
District here since 1990 when Masa's long-time maître d' opened his own place, which he calls a "San Francisco brasserie." This categorizes the contemporary American cooking somewhat, but the decor defies description. It could be interpreted as anything from a parody of an ancient temple to a futuristic space war. *500 Jackson St., tel. 415/296–8555. Reservations advised. Dress: informal. AE, DC, MC, V. No lunch Sat. Closed Thanksgiving, Christmas, New Year's Day. Valet parking at night. Expensive.*

Nob Hill **Ritz-Carlton Restaurant and Dining Room.**
★ There are two distinctively different places to eat in this neoclassical Nob Hill showplace. The Restaurant, a cheerful, informal spot with a large patio for outdoor dining, serves breakfast, lunch, dinner, and a Sunday jazz brunch from spring to fall; the Dining Room, formal and elegant with a harpist playing, serves only two- to five-course dinners (uniquely priced by the course, not by the item). And except for the chef's five-course tasting menu, there's a wide selection of choices at the latter. Both rooms, however, present a superb version of Northern California cooking that is basically American utilizing local products and adding Mediterranean and Asian overtones. The culinary master behind this is chef Gary Danko, who developed the menu for the Restaurant and then went on to win four-star reviews as executive chef of the Dining Room. *600 Stockton St., tel. 415/296–7465. Reservations advised. Dress: informal in the Restaurant, jacket and tie required in the Dining Room. AE, DC, MC, V. The Dining Room closed Sun. Valet parking. Moderate-Expensive.*

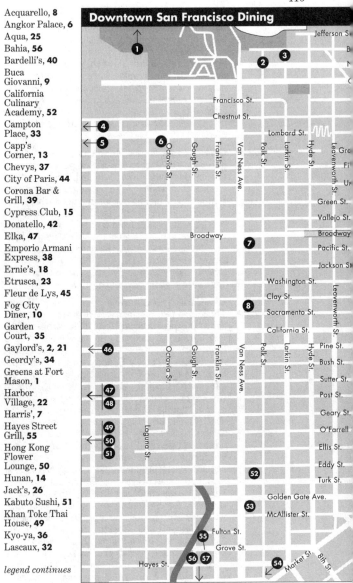

Downtown San Francisco Dining

Le Central, **31**
MacArthur Park, **17**
Masa's, **30**
Maykedeh, **12**
McCormick & Kuleto's, **3**
Moose's, **11**
North India, **5**
Pacific Heights Bar & Grill, **46**
Postrio, **43**
Ristorante Parma, **4**
Ritz Carlton Restaurant and Dining Room, **26**
S. Asimakopoulos Cafe, **41**
Sam's Grill, **29**
Sanppo, **48**
Square One, **16**
Splendido's, **20**
Stars, **53**
Tadich Grill, **24**
Thepin, **57**
Wu Kong, **23**
Yamato, **28**
Yank Sing, **19**
Zuni Cafe Grill, **54**

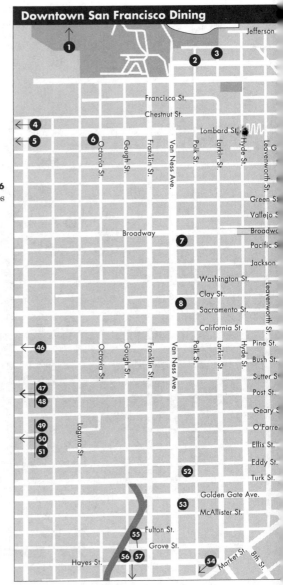

Downtown San Francisco Dining

Beach St.

North St.

Embarcadero

Bay St.

Francisco St.

Chestnut St.

Lombard St.

Columbus Ave

Greenwich St. **9**

Filbert St.

Union St. **11**

St. **12**

St.

13

Columbus Ave

way Tunnel

St.

on St.

10

Front St.

Embarcadero

Davis St.

15 **14**

18 **16**

17

Montgomery St.

Sansome St.

Battery St.

19

Drumm St.

Davis St.

20

Front St.

21

22

Stewart St.

Taylor St.

Mason St.

Powell St.

Stockton St.

Grant Ave.

Kearney St.

26

25

24 *AE*

Main St.

Spear St.

23

Jones St.

27 **28**

30

29

32 **31**

45

33 **34**

44 **43** **42**

AE

AE

Beale St.

Fremont St.

1st St.

Market St. **35**

36 New Montgomery St.

2nd St.

Hawthorn St.

y St.

rell St.

t.

40 **38**

39

3rd St.

St.

t.

37 4th St.

Mission St.

5th St.

Howard St.

Folsom St.

Harrison St.

Bryant St.

6th St.

0   1/4 mile

0   250 meters

7th St.

41

N

KEY

AE American Express Office

Union Square **Postrio.** This is the place for those who want to
★ see and be seen: There's always a chance to
catch a glimpse of some celebrity, including
Postrio's owner, superchef Wolfgang Puck, who
periodically commutes from Los Angeles to
make an appearance in the restaurant's open
kitchen. A stunning three-level bar and dining
area is highlighted by palm trees and museum-
quality contemporary paintings. The food is
Puckish Californian with Mediterranean and
Asian overtones, emphasizing pastas, grilled
seafood, and house-baked breads. A substantial
breakfast and bar menu (with great pizza) are
served here, too. *545 Post St., tel. 415/776–7825.
Reservations advised. Jacket and tie suggested.
AE, DC, MC, V. Valet parking. Expensive–
Very Expensive.*

★ **Campton Place.** This elegant, ultrasophisticated small hotel put new American cooking
on the local culinary map. Chef Jan Birnbaum
carries on the innovative traditions of opening
chef Bradley Ogden with great aplomb and
has added his own touches from breakfast
and Sunday brunch (one of the best in town)
through the dinner hours. A bar menu offers
some samplings of appetizers, plus a caviar extravaganza. *340 Stockton St., tel. 415/955–5555.
Reservations suggested, 2 wks in advance on
weekends. Jacket required at dinner, tie requested. AE, DC, MC, V. Valet parking. Expensive.*

Chinese

For nearly a century, Chinese restaurants in
San Francisco were confined to Chinatown and
the cooking was largely an Americanized version of peasant-style Cantonese. The past few
decades, however, have seen an influx of restaurants representing the wide spectrum of Chinese cuisine: the subtly seasoned fare of Canton,
the hot and spicy cooking of Hunan and
Szechuan, the northern style of Peking, where
meat and dumplings replace seafood and rice as
staples, and, more recently, some more esoteric
cooking, such as Hakka and Chao Chow. The
current rage seems to be the high-style influence of Hong Kong. These restaurants are now

American Express offers Travelers Cheques built for two.

American Express® Cheques *for Two*. The first Travelers Cheques that allow either of you to use them because both of you have signed them. And only one of you needs to be present to purchase them.

Cheques *for Two* are accepted anywhere regular American Express Travelers Cheques are, which is just about everywhere. So stop by your bank, AAA* or any American Express Travel Service Office and ask for Cheques *for Two*.

AMERICAN EXPRESS **Travelers Cheques** ®

scattered throughout the city, leaving China-town for the most part to the tourists.

Embarcadero North ★

Harbor Village. Classic Cantonese cooking, dim sum lunches, and fresh seafood from the restaurant's own tanks are the hallmarks of this 400-seat branch of a Hong Kong establishment, which sent five of its master chefs to San Francisco to supervise the kitchen. The setting is opulent, with Chinese antiques and teak furnishings. *4 Embarcadero Center, tel. 415/781–8833. Reservations not accepted for lunch on weekends. Dress: informal. AE, DC, MC, V. Validated parking in Embarcadero Center Garage (free at night and on weekends). Moderate.*

Embarcadero South

Wu Kong. Tucked away in the splashy Art Deco Rincon Center, Wu Kong features the cuisine of Shanghai and Canton. Specialties include dim sum; braised yellow fish; and the incredible vegetarian goose, one of the Asian city's famous mock dishes, created from paper-thin layers of dried bean-curd sheets and mushrooms. *101 Spear St., tel. 415/957–9300. Reservations advised. Dress: informal. AE, DC, MC, V. Validated parking at Rincon Center garage. Moderate.*

Financial District

Yank Sing. This tea house has grown by leaps and branches with the popularity of dim sum. The Battery Street location seats 300 and the older, smaller Stevenson Street site has recently been rebuilt in high-tech style. *427 Battery St., tel. 415/362–1640; 49 Stevenson St., tel. 415/495–4510. Reservations advised. Dress: informal. AE, MC, V. No dinner. Stevenson site closed weekends. Inexpensive.*

Hunan. Henry Chung's first café on Kearny Street had only six tables, but his Hunanese cooking merited six stars from critics nationwide. He has now opened this larger place on Sansome Street; it's equally plain but has 250 seats. Smoked dishes are a specialty, and Henry guarantees no MSG. *924 Sansome St., tel. 415/956–7727. Reservations advised. Dress: informal. AE, DC, MC, V. Inexpensive.*

Richmond ★

Hong Kong Flower Lounge. Many Chinaphiles swear that this outpost of a famous Asian restaurant chain serves the best Cantonese food in town. The seafood is spectacular, as is the dim sum. *5322 Geary Blvd., tel. 415/668–8998. Reservations advised. Dress: informal. AE, MC, V. Moderate.*

French

French cooking has gone in and out of vogue in San Francisco since the extravagant days of the Bonanza Kings. A renaissance of the classic haute cuisine occurred during the 1960s, but recently a number of these restaurants closed. Meanwhile, nouvelle cuisine went in and out of fashion, and the big draw now is the bistro or brasserie.

Civic Center **California Culinary Academy.** This historic theater houses one of the most highly regarded professional cooking schools in the United States. Watch the student chefs at work on the double-tier stage while you dine on classic French cooking. Prix-fixe meals and bountiful buffets are served in the main dining room, and there's an informal grill on the first floor. *625 Polk St., tel. 415/771–3500. Reservations advised (2–4 wks for Fri.–night buffet). Jacket and tie requested, but not required. AE, DC, MC, V. Closed weekends and major holidays. Moderate–Expensive.*

Financial District **Le Central.** This is the quintessential bistro: noisy and crowded, with nothing subtle about the cooking. But the garlicky pâtés, leeks vinaigrette, cassoulet, and grilled blood sausage with crisp french fries keep the crowds coming. *453 Bush St., tel. 415/391–2233. Reservations advised. Dress: informal. AE, MC, V. Closed Sun. and major holidays. Moderate.*

North Beach **Ernie's.** This famous old-timer recently had a face-lift and now conjures up innovative light versions of French classics. Even so, Ernie's is still steeped with the aura of Gay Nineties San Francisco and is about the only place in town that offers tableside service. You will pay dearly for dinner, but the prix fixe, three-course lunch is a bargain. *847 Montgomery St., tel. 415/397–5969. Reservations advised. Jacket required. AE, DC, MC, V. No lunch Sat.–Mon. Closed major holidays. Valet parking. Very Expensive.*

Union Square
★ **Masa's.** Chef Julian Serrano carries on the tradition of the late Masa Kobayashi. In fact, some Masa regulars even say the cooking is better. The artistry of the presentation is as important as the food itself in this pretty, flower-filled dining spot in the Vintage Court Hotel. *648 Bush St., tel. 415/989-7154. Reservations accepted up to 3 mos in advance. Jacket required. AE, DC, MC, V. No lunch. Closed Sun., Mon., 1st week in July, last week in Dec., 1st week in Jan. Valet parking. Very Expensive.*

★ **Fleur de Lys.** The creative cooking of chef-partner Hubert Keller is drawing rave reviews to this romantic spot that some now consider the best French restaurant in town. The menu changes constantly, but such dishes as lobster soup with lemongrass are a signature. The intimate dining room, like a sheikh's tent, is encased with hundreds of yards of paisley. *777 Sutter St., tel. 415/673-7779. Reservations on weekends advised 2 wks in advance. Jacket required. AE, DC, MC, V. No lunch. Closed Sun., Thanksgiving, Christmas, New Year's Day. Valet parking. Very Expensive.*

City of Paris. The hit of the 1992–93 theater season was not a play, but this new bistro smack in the middle of theater row. Every effort was made to replicate a typical Parisian bistro—jammed-together tables, an open kitchen where plump chickens slowly turn on an ornate cast-iron and brass rotisserie, and such bistro classics as *petit salé* (pork pickled in brine), *gite gite* (skirt steak with frites), and French onion soup. But unlike the City of Lights, the prices (same at lunch and dinner) are remarkably low. *101 Shannon Alley (off Geary St. between Jones and Taylor), tel. 415/441-4442. AE, MC, V. Closed Christmas and July 4. Valet parking. Moderate–Inexpensive.*

Greek and Middle Eastern

The foods of Greece and the Middle East have much in common: a preponderance of lamb and eggplant dishes, a wide-spread use of phyllo pastry, and an abundance of pilaf.

North Beach **Maykadeh.** Here you'll find authentic Persian cooking in a setting so elegant that the modest

check comes as a great surprise. Lamb dishes
with rice are the specialties. *470 Green St., tel.
415/362–8286. Reservations advised. Dress: informal. MC, V. Valet parking at night. Moderate–Inexpensive.*

South of **S. Asimakopoulos Cafe.** Terrific Greek food at
Market reasonable prices keeps the crowds waiting for
seats at the counter or at bare-topped tables in
this storefront café. The menu is large and varied, but lamb dishes are the stars. Convenient to
showplace Square. *288 Connecticut, Potrero
Hill, tel. 415/552–8789. No reservations. Dress:
informal. AE, MC, V. No lunch weekends.
Closed major holidays. Moderate–Inexpensive.*

Indian

The following restaurants serve the cuisine of
northern India, which is more subtly seasoned
and not as hot as its southern counterparts.
They also specialize in succulent meats and
crispy breads from the clay-lined tandoori oven.

Northern **Gaylord's.** A vast selection of mildly spiced
Waterfront northern Indian food is offered here, along with
and meats and breads from the tandoori ovens and a
Embarcadero wide range of vegetarian dishes. The dining
rooms are elegantly appointed with Indian
paintings and gleaming silver service. The
Ghirardelli Square location offers bay views.
*Ghirardelli Sq., tel. 415/771–8822; Embarcade-
ro 1, tel. 415/397–7775. Reservations advised.
Dress: informal. AE, DC, MC, V. No lunch
Sun. at Embarcadero. Closed Thanksgiving,
Christmas. Validated parking at Ghirardelli
Sq. garage and Embarcadero Center garage.
Moderate.*

Pacific **North India.** Small and cozy, this restaurant has
Heights a more limited menu and hotter seasoning than
Gaylord's. Both tandoori dishes and curries are
served, plus a range of breads and appetizers.
Everything is cooked to order. *3131 Webster St.,
tel. 415/931–1556. Reservations advised. Dress:
informal. AE, DC, MC, V. No lunch weekends.
Parking behind restaurant. Moderate.*

Italian

Italian food in San Francisco spans the "boot" from the mild cooking of northern Italy to the spicy cuisine of the south. Then there is the style indigenous to San Francisco, known as North Beach Italian—such dishes as *cioppino* (a fisherman's stew) and Joe's special (a mélange of eggs, spinach, and ground beef).

Embarcadero South ★ **Etrusca.** The ancient Etruscan civilization inspired this popular showplace in Rincon Center. Onyx chandeliers cast a warm glow on Siena gold walls, terrazzo floors, and ceiling frescoes. The dishes from the giant wood-fire oven that dominates the open kitchen, however, recall modern Tuscany more than ancient Etruria. A bar menu is also available. *Rincon Center, 101 Spear St., tel. 415/777-0330. Reservations advised. Dress: informal. AE, MC, V. No lunch weekends. Closed Thanksgiving, Christmas, New Year's Day. Validated parking in Rincon Center garage, valet service at night. Moderate.*

Marina **Ristorante Parma.** This is a warm, wonderfully honest trattoria with excellent food at modest prices. The antipasti tray, with a dozen unusual items, is one of the best in town, and the pastas and veal are exceptional. Don't pass up the spinach gnocchi when it is offered. *3314 Steiner St., tel. 415/567-0500. Reservations advised. Dress: informal. AE, MC, V. No lunch. Closed Sun. and some major holidays. Moderate.*

Midtown ★ **Acquarello.** This exquisite restaurant is a venture of the former chef and former maître d' at Donatello. The service and food are exemplary, and the menu covers the full range of Italian cuisine, from northern Italy to the tip of the boot. Desserts are exceptional. *1722 Sacramento St., tel. 415/567-5432. Reservations advised. Dress: informal. DC, MC, V. No lunch. Closed Sun.-Mon. Expensive-Moderate.*

North Beach ★ **Buca Giovanni.** Giovanni Leoni showcases the dishes of his birthplace, the Serchio Valley in Tuscany, and grows many of the vegetables and herbs used in his recipes at his Mendocino County ranch. Pastas made on the premises are a specialty, and the calamari salad is one of the best around. The subterranean dining room is cozy and romantic. *800 Greenwich St., tel. 415/776–7766. Reservations advised. Dress: informal. AE, DC, MC, V. No lunch. Closed Sun. and most major holidays. Moderate.*

★ **Capp's Corner.** One of the last of the family-style trattorias, diners sit elbow to elbow at long oilcloth-covered tables to feast on bountiful, well-prepared five-course dinners. For calorie-counters or the budget-minded, a shorter dinner includes a tureen of minestrone, salad, and pasta. *1600 Powell St., tel. 415/989–2589. Reservations advised. Dress: informal. DC, MC, V. No lunch weekends. Closed Thanksgiving, Christmas. Credit off meal check for parking in garage across the street. Inexpensive.*

Union Square **Donatello.** Long touted as the city's *primo ristorante italiano*, Donatello's star began to wane in the early 1990s until a new kitchen team—veteran chef Patrizio Sacchetto and the noted cookbook author Carol Field as consultant—restored the culinary glitter. Sacchetto's cooking is from the north of Italy (principally Piedmont), with admirable risotti and remarkable multicolored striped pastas at center stage. Field's breads and *dolci* are straight from heaven. Unchanged are the intimate dining rooms, exquisitely appointed with silk-paneled walls, paintings, and tapestries. *Post and Mason Sts., tel. 415/441–7182. Reservations advised. Jacket required. AE, DC, MC, V. No lunch. Validated parking in hotel garage. Expensive–Very Expensive.*

Emporio Armani Express. Designer Giorgio Armani is best known for his clothing, but with little fanfare he has also designed some smart little cafés within his boutiques in London, Costa Mesa, Seoul—and now San Francisco. Here, under the Pantheon-like dome of a former bank building, tables and banquettes are set on a mezzanine overlooking the store's main floor. The food is exquisite northern Italian fare uncluttered by clichés. For antipasti, try the *breseaoloa* (paper-thin slices of air-dried beef) tossed with baby greens and artichoke hearts, or the grilled polenta, crowned with sautéed wild mushrooms. The pastas are also recommended, and the desserts—often the weak spot of an Italian meal—are superb. *1 Grant Ave.,* tel. *415/677–9010. Reservations advised. Dress: informal. AE, DC, MC, V. Moderate.*

Japanese

To understand a Japanese menu, you should be familiar with the basic types of cooking: *yaki,* marinated and grilled foods; *tempura,* fish and vegetables deep-fried in a light batter; *udon* and *soba,* noodle dishes; *domburi,* meats and vegetables served over rice; *ramen,* noodles served in broth; and *nabemono,* meals cooked in one pot, often at the table. Sushi bars are extremely popular in San Francisco; most offer a selection of *sushi,* vinegared rice with fish or vegetables, and *sashimi,* raw fish. Western seating refers to conventional tables and chairs; *tatami* seating is on mats at low tables.

Chinatown **Yamato.** The city's oldest Japanese restaurant is by far its most beautiful, with inlaid wood, painted panels, a meditation garden, and a pool. Both Western and tatami seating, in private shoji-screened rooms, are offered, along with a fine sushi bar. Come primarily for the atmosphere; the menu is somewhat limited, and more adventurous dining can be found elsewhere. *717 California St., tel. 415/397–3456. Reservations advised. AE, DC, MC, V. No lunch weekends. Closed Mon., Thanksgiving, Christmas, New Year's Day. Moderate.*

Financial **Kyo-ya.** Rarely replicated outside Japan, the re-
District fined experience of dining in a fine Japanese restaurant has been introduced with extraordinary authenticity at this new showplace within the Sheraton-Palace Hotel. In Japan, a *kyo-ya* is a nonspecialized restaurant that serves a wide range of food types. And at this Kyo-ya, the range is spectacular—encompassing tempuras, one-pot dishes, deep-fried and grilled meats, not to mention a choice of some three dozen sushi selections. The lunch menu is more limited than at dinner but does offer a *shokado,* a sampler of four classic dishes encased in a handsome lacquered lunch box. *Sheraton-Palace Hotel, 2 New Montgomery St., at Market St., tel. 415/ 546–5000. Reservations advised. Dress: informal. AE, DC, MC, V. Closed weekends and Christmas. Moderate–Expensive.*

Japantown   **Sanppo.** This small place has an enormous selection of almost every type of Japanese food: yakis, nabemono dishes, domburi, udon, and soba, not to mention feather-light tempura and interesting side dishes. Western seating only. *1702 Post St., tel. 415/346-3486. No reservations. Dress: informal. No credit cards. Closed Mon. and major holidays. Validated parking in Japan Center garage. Inexpensive.*

Richmond   **Kabuto Sushi.** For one of the most spectacular acts in town, head out Geary Boulevard past Japantown to tiny Kabuto. Here, behind his black-lacquered counter, master chef Sachio Kojima flashes his knives with the grace of a samurai warrior to prepare sushi and sashimi of exceptional quality. Traditional Japanese dinners are also served in the adjoining dining room with both Western seating and, in a shoji-screened area, *tatami* seating. *5116 Geary Blvd., tel. 415/752-5652. Reservations advised for dinner. Dress: informal. MC, V. No lunch. Closed Mon., Thanksgiving, Christmas, New Year's Day. Moderate.*

Mediterranean

In its climate and topography, its agriculture and viticulture, and the orientation of many of its early settlers, northern California resembles the Mediterranean region. But until quite recently no restaurant billed itself as "Mediterranean." Those that do so now primarily offer a mix of southern French and northern Italian food, but some include accents from Spain, Greece, and more distant ports of call.

Civic Center   **Zuni Cafe Grill.** Zuni's Italian-Mediterranean
★   menu and its unpretentious atmosphere pack in the crowds from early morning to late evening. A balcony dining area overlooks the large bar, where both shellfish and drinks are dispensed. A second dining room houses the giant pizza oven and grill. Even the hamburgers have an Italian accent: They're served on herbed focaccia buns. *1658 Market St., tel. 415/552-2522. Reservations advised. Dress: informal. AE, MC, V. Closed Mon., Thanksgiving, Christmas. Moderate-Expensive.*

Embarcadero North ★ **Square One.** Chef Joyce Goldstein introduces an ambitious new menu daily, with dishes based on the classic cooking of the Mediterranean countries, although she sometimes strays to Asia and Latin America. The dining room, with its views of the open kitchen and the Golden Gateway commons, is an understated setting for some of the finest food in town. A bar menu is available. *190 Pacific Ave., tel. 415/788–1110. Reservations advised. Dress: informal. AE, DC, MC, V. No lunch weekends. Closed major holidays. Valet parking in evenings. Expensive–Moderate.*

Splendido's. Mediterranean cooking is the focus at this handsome new restaurant. Diners here are transported to the coast of southern France or northern Italy by the pleasant decor. Among the many winners are the shellfish soup and warm goat-cheese and ratatouille salad. Desserts are truly *splendido*. A bar menu is available. *Embarcadero 4, tel. 415/986–3222. Reservations advised. Dress: informal. AE, DC, MC, V. No lunch weekends. Closed major holidays. Validated parking at Embarcadero Center garage. Moderate.*

North Beach ★ **Moose's.** From opening day in 1992, Ed Moose's new restaurant was destined to become the city's top celebrity hangout, especially for the politicians and media types who have followed him from his former digs at Washington Square Bar & Grill just across the large tree-shaded plaza. Along with a host of local luminaries, Tom Brokaw, Walter Cronkite, Tom Wolfe, and Senator Dianne Feinstein head for Moose's when they're in town. And the food impresses as much as the clientele: A Mediterranean-inspired menu highlights innovative appetizers (such as a "Napoleon" of layered eggplant and mozzarella), pastas (including tortellini stuffed with mashed sweet potatoes), seafood, and grills. The surroundings are classic and comfortable, with views of Washington Square and Russian Hill from a front café area and, in the rear facing the open kitchen, counter seats for singles. There's live music at night and a fine Sunday brunch. *1652 Stockton St., tel. 415/989–7800. Reservations required several wks in advance.*

Dress: informal. AE, DC, MC, V. Valet parking. Moderate.

Union Square **Geordy's.** Many chic patrons of Postrio, where Geordy Murphy was manager, have followed him to his own spot on Tillman Place, which once housed the landmark Templebar restaurant. But the long narrow barroom with two rows of tables has been totally revamped in an understated contemporary style. The innovative Mediterranean-style cooking is the work of Charles Solomon, most recently sous-chef of New York's celebrated Bouley's. He has a penchant for combining seafood with pasta: ravioli stuffed with crayfish in a lobster consommé, monkfish tails with gnocchi, lobster and saffron fettuccine. But the star entrée on the menu may be the roast chicken stuffed with brioche, foie gras, and chicken livers. *1 Tillman Pl. (off Grant Ave., between Post and Sutters Sts.), tel. 415/ 362–3175. Reservations advised. Dress: informal. AE, DC, MC, V. Closed Sun. Valet parking at night. Moderate.*

Lascaux. Despite its Gallic name (after the primitive caves in France), the cuisine at this smart new restaurant is primarily Mediterranean, with a contemporary Italian accent. Of particular note are the appetizers (such as sun-dried tomato and mascarpone torta, or the various takes on polenta), split-roasted meats, and grilled seafood with zesty sauces. A huge fireplace cheers the romantically lighted subterranean dining room. Live jazz is offered at night. *248 Sutter St., tel. 415/391–1555. Reservations advised. Dress: informal. AE, DC, MC, V. No lunch weekend. Closed Thanksgiving, Christmas, New Year's Day. Moderate.*

Mexican/Latin American

In spite of San Francisco's Mexican heritage, until recently most south-of-the-border eateries were locked into the Cal-Mex taco-enchilada-mashed-beans syndrome. But now some newer places offer a broader spectrum of Mexican and Latin American cooking.

Civic Center **Bahia.** An evening at this festive Brazilian café is like a quick trip to the tropics. Amid lush foliage, bold paintings, and the beat of the samba, you can feast on all the great Brazilian classics like *feijoada* (pork and black-bean stew), *bobo de camarão* (shrimp in coconut milk), and creamy chicken croquettes. In the early evening, there's a tapas bar. On Thursday, Friday, and Saturday nights, the music is live. And just down the street is Bahia's nightclub, which gyrates with the lambada until the wee hours. *41 Franklin St., tel. 415/626–3306. Reservations advised. Dress: informal. MC, V. ModerateInexpensive.*

South of Market **Chevys.** This first San Francisco branch of a popular Mexican minichain is decked out with funky neon signs and "El Machino" turning out flour tortillas. "Stop gringo food" is the motto here, and the emphasis is on the freshest ingredients and sauces. Of note are the fabulous fajitas and the grilled quail and seafood. *4th and Howard Sts., tel. 415/543–8060. Reservations accepted only for parties of 8 or more. Dress: informal. AE, MC, V. Closed Thanksgiving, Christmas. Validated parking evenings and weekends at garage under bldg. (enter from Minna St.). Inexpensive.*

Union Square ★ **Corona Bar & Grill.** The ever-changing menu offers light versions of regional Mexican dishes. Corona's paella, laden with shellfish and calamari, is sensational, as is the chocolate-coated flan. The atmosphere is a mix of old San Francisco (pressed tin ceilings and an antique bar) and old Mexico (hand-painted masks and Aztec motifs). *88 Cyril Magnin St., tel. 415/392–5500. Reservations advised. Dress: informal. AE, DC, MC, V. No lunch Sun. Closed Thanksgiving, Christmas. Moderate.*

Old San Francisco

Several of the city's landmark restaurants just don't fit neatly into any ethnic category. Some might call them Continental or French or even American. But dating back to the turn of the century or earlier, these places all exude the traditions and aura of old San Francisco. The oldest one of them all, Tadich Grill, is listed under Seafood.

Financial District ★

Garden Court. After a massive, two-year, multi-million-dollar renovation, the Garden Court of the Sheraton Palace has reemerged as the ultimate old San Francisco experience. From breakfast through lunch, teatime, and the early dinner hours, light splashes through the $7 million stained-glass ceiling against the towering Ionic columns and crystal chandeliers. The classic European menu highlights many famous dishes devised by Palace chefs during the early years of this century, and the extravagant Sunday buffet brunch again takes center stage as one of the city's great traditions. *Market and New Montgomery Sts., tel. 415/546–5000. Reservations advised. Dress: informal. AE, DC, MC, V. Expensive.*

Jack's. Little has changed in more than 100 years at this bankers' and brokers' favorite. The menu is extensive, but regulars opt for the simple fare—steaks, chops, seafood, and stews. The dining room, like the food, has an old-fashioned, no-nonsense aura, and private upstairs rooms are available for top-secret meetings. *615 Sacramento St., tel. 415/986–9854. Reservations advised. Jacket requested. AE. No lunch weekends. Closed major holidays. Moderate.*

Union Square

Bardelli's. Founded in 1906 as Charles' Oyster House, this turn-of-the-century showplace boasts vaulted ceilings, massive marble columns, and stained glass. The traditional menu mixes French, Italian, and American fare with superb fresh seafood. *243 O'Farrell St., tel. 415/982–0243. Reservations accepted. Dress: informal. AE, DC, MC, V. No lunch Sat. Closed Sun. Validated parking at Downtown Center garage. Moderate.*

Seafood

Like all port cities, San Francisco takes pride in its seafood, even though less than half the fish served here is from local waters. In winter and spring look for the fresh Dungeness crab, best served cracked with mayonnaise. In summer, feast upon Pacific salmon, even though imported varieties are available year-round. A recent development is the abundance of unusual oysters from West Coast beds and an outburst of oyster bars.

Civic Center **Hayes Street Grill.** Eight to 15 different kinds of
★ seafood are chalked on the blackboard each night at this extremely popular restaurant. The fish is served simply grilled, with a choice of sauces ranging from tartar to a spicy Szechuan peanut concoction. Appetizers are unusual, and desserts are lavish. *320 Hayes St., tel. 415/863–5545. Reservations should be made precisely 1 wk in advance. Dress: informal. AE, DC, MC, V. No lunch weekends. Closed major holidays. Moderate.*

Financial **Aqua.** This quietly elegant and ultrafashionable
District spot is possibly the city's most important sea-
★ food restaurant ever. Chef-owner George Morrone has a supremely original talent for creating contemporary versions of French, Italian, and American classics: Expect mussel, crab, or lobster soufflés; lobster gnocchi with lobster sauce; shrimp and corn madeleines strewn in a salad; and ultrarare ahi paired with foie gras. Desserts are miniature museum pieces. *252 California St., tel. 415/956–9662. Reservations essential. Dress: informal. AE, DC, MC, V. No lunch Sat. Closed Sun. Valet parking at night. Expensive.*

Sam's Grill. Sam's and Tadich (*see below*) are two of the city's oldest restaurants and so popular for lunch that you must arrive before 11:30 to get a table. No frills here. The aura is starkly old-fashioned; some booths are enclosed and curtained. Although the menu is extensive and varied, those in the know stick with the fresh local seafood and East Coast shellfish. *374 Bush St., tel. 415/421–0594. Reservations accepted only for parties of 6 or more. Dress: informal. AE, DC, MC, V. Closed weekends and holidays. Moderate.*

Tadich Grill. Owners and locations have changed many times since this old-timer opened during the gold-rush era, but the 19th-century atmosphere remains, as does the kitchen's special way with seafood. Seating at the counter or in private booths; long lines for a table at lunchtime. *240 California St., tel. 415/391–2373. No reservations. Dress: informal. MC, V. Closed Sun. and holidays. Moderate.*

Japantown **Elka.** One of the most talked-about chefs in town
nowadays is Elka Gilmore. Her innovative East-
meets-West seafood cuisine has had the critics
turning cartwheels since 1992 when she arrived
at the Miyako Hotel, which rechristened its
handsome multilevel dining room in her honor.
For a starter, Elka's "Japanese box filled with
small seafood dishes" is a must. It's a small
wooden cabinet with nooks and crannies that
conceal the changing whims of the chef—perhaps a dab of sturgeon mousse, or a scallop gar-
nished with foie gras, or a crab cake with corn
relish. The artfully presented entrées range
from Japanese buckwheat noodles with caviar
to roasted fillet of sea bass topped with eggplant
purée. But for desserts, Elka looks to the West
with the likes of apple pie and ice cream. *1611
Post St., tel. 415/922–7788. Reservations advised. Dress: informal. AE, MC, V. Expensive–Moderate.*

Northern **McCormick & Kuleto's.** This new seafood empo-
Waterfront rium in Ghirardelli Square is a visitor's dream
come true: a fabulous view of the bay from every
seat in the house; an old San Francisco atmosphere; and some 30 varieties of fish and shellfish
prepared in some 70 globe-circling ways, from
tacos, pot stickers, and fish cakes to grills, pastas, and stew. The food does have its ups and
downs, however, but even on foggy days you can
count on the view. *Ghirardelli Sq., tel. 415/929–
1730. Reservations advised. Dress: informal.
AE, DC, MC, V. Validated parking in Ghirardelli Sq. garage. Moderate.*

Pacific **Pacific Heights Bar & Grill.** This is unquestiona-
Heights bly the best oyster bar in town, with at least a
dozen varieties available each day and knowledgeable shuckers to explain the mollusks' origins. In the small dining rooms, grilled seafood
and shellfish stews head the bill of fare. Paella is
a house specialty. *2001 Fillmore St., tel. 415/
567–3337. Reservations advised. Dress: informal. AE, DC, MC, V. No lunch. Closed
Thanksgiving, Christmas Eve, and Christmas.
Moderate.*

Southeast Asian

In recent years San Franciscans have seen tremendous growth in the numbers of restaurants specializing in the foods of Thailand, Vietnam, and, most recently, Cambodia. The cuisines of these countries share many features, and one characteristic in particular: The cooking is always spicy and often very hot.

Civic Center **Thepin.** It seems as if there's a Thai restaurant on every block now, but this is the jewel in the crown. The stylish dining room sparkles with linen napery, fresh flowers, Thai artworks, and a wine list that surpasses the Asian norm. Notable are the duck dishes and the curries, each prepared with its own mixture of freshly blended spices. *298 Gough St., tel. 415/863–9335. Reservations advised. Dress: informal. AE, MC, V. No lunch weekends. Closed major holidays. Moderate–Inexpensive.*

Marina **Angkor Palace.** This is one of the loveliest Cambodian restaurants in town and also the most conveniently located for visitors. The extensive family-style menu offers such exotic fare as fish-and-coconut mousse baked in banana leaves. You'll have questions, of course, but you'll find the staff eager to explain the contents of the menu. *1769 Lombard St., tel. 415/931–2830. Reservations advised. Dress: informal. AE, MC, V. No lunch. Closed Christmas. Inexpensive.*

Richmond District
★ **Khan Toke Thai House.** The city's first Thai restaurant has a lovely dining room, furnished with low tables and cushions, and a garden view. The six-course dinners, with two entrées from an extensive choice, provide a delicious introduction to Thai cooking. (The seasoning will be mild, unless you request it hot.) Classical Thai dancing on Sunday. *5937 Geary Blvd., tel. 415/668–6654. Reservations advised. Dress: informal. AE, DC, MC, V. No lunch. Closed Thanksgiving, Christmas. Moderate–Inexpensive.*

Steak Houses

Although San Francisco traditionally has not been a meat-and-potatoes town, the popularity of steak is on the rise.

Midtown
★
Harris'. Ann Harris knows her beef. She grew up on a Texas cattle ranch and was married to the late Jack Harris of Harris Ranch fame. In her own elegant restaurant she serves some of the best dry-aged steaks in town, but don't overlook the grilled seafood or poultry. There is also an extensive bar menu. *2100 Van Ness Ave., tel. 415/673–1888. Reservations recommended. Dress: informal. AE, DC, MC, V. Lunch on Wed. only. Closed Christmas, New Year's Day. Valet parking. Expensive.*

Vegetarian

Aside from the restaurant mentioned below, vegetarians should also consider Gaylord's (*see* Indian restaurants, *above*), which offers a wide variety of meatless dishes from the Hindu cuisine.

Marina
★
Greens at Fort Mason. This beautiful restaurant with its bay views is a favorite with carnivores as well as vegetarians. Owned and operated by the Tassajara Zen Center of Carmel Valley, the restaurant offers a wide, eclectic, and creative spectrum of meatless cooking, and the bread promises nirvana. Dinners are à la carte on weeknights, but only a five-course prix-fixe dinner is served on Friday and Saturday. *Bldg. A, Fort Mason, tel. 415/771–6222. Reservations advised. Dress: informal. MC, V. No dinner Sun. Closed Mon., Thanksgiving, Christmas, New Year's Day. Public parking at Fort Mason Center. Moderate.*

5 Lodging

By Laura Del
Rosso

*Laura Del
Rosso is San
Francisco
bureau chief
for* Travel
Weekly, *a
news
magazine for
the travel
industry, and
often writes
about San
Francisco for
other
publications.*

Few cities in the United States can rival San Francisco's variety in lodging. There are plush hotels ranked among the finest in the world, renovated older buildings that have the charm of Europe, bed-and-breakfasts in the city's Victorian "Painted Ladies," and the popular chain hotels found in most cities in the United States.

One of the brightest spots in the lodging picture is the transformation of handsome early 20th-century downtown high rises into small, distinctive hotels that offer personal service and European-style ambience. Another is the recent addition of ultradeluxe modern hotels such as the Nikko, Pan Pacific, ANA, and Mandarin Oriental, which promote their attentive Asian-style hospitality. On top of those offerings are the dozens of popular chain hotels that continually undergo face-lifts and additions to keep up with the competition.

The **San Francisco Convention and Visitors Bureau** (tel. 415/391–2001) publishes a free lodging guide with a map and listing of all hotels. Send $2 for postage and handling to Box 429097, San Francisco 94142–9097.

Because San Francisco is one of the top destinations in the United States for tourists as well as business travelers and convention goers, reservations are always advised, especially during the May–October peak season.

San Francisco's geography makes it conveniently compact. No matter their location, the hotels listed below are on or close to public transportation lines. Some properties on Lombard Street and in the Civic Center area have free parking, but a car is more a hindrance than an asset in San Francisco.

Although not as high as the rates in New York, San Francisco hotel prices may come as a surprise to travelers from less urban areas. Average rates for double rooms downtown and at the wharf are in the $110 range. Adding to the expense is the city's 11% transient occupancy tax, which can significantly boost the cost of a lengthy stay. The good news is that because of the hotel building boom of the late 1980s, there is now an oversupply of rooms, which has led to much discounting of prices. Check for special rates and packages when making reservations.

If you are looking for truly budget accommodations (under $50), consider the Adelaide Inn (*see* Union Square/Downtown, *below*) and the **YMCA Central Branch.** *220 Golden Gate Ave., 94102, tel. 415/885-0460. 102 rooms, 3 with bath. Facilities: health club, pool, sauna. MC, V.*

An alternative to hotels and motels is staying in private homes and apartments, available through **American Family Inn/Bed & Breakfast San Francisco** (Box 420009, San Francisco 94142, tel. 415/931-3083), **Bed & Breakfast International-San Francisco** (Box 282910, San Francisco 94128-2910, tel. 415/969-1690 or 800/872-4500, fax 415/696-1699), and **American Property Exchange** (170 Page St., San Francisco 94102, tel. 415/863-8484 or 800/747-7784).

Category	Cost*
Very Expensive	over $175
Expensive	$110-$175
Moderate	$75-$110
Inexpensive	under $75

All prices are for a standard double room, excluding 11% tax.

The following credit card abbreviations are used: AE, American Express; DC, Diners Club; MC, MasterCard; V, Visa.

Union Square/Downtown

The largest variety and greatest concentration of hotels are in the city's downtown hub, Union Square, where hotel guests find the best shopping, the theater district, and transportation to every spot in San Francisco.

Very Expensive ★ **Campton Place Kempinski.** Steps away from Union Square is one of San Francisco's most elegant and highly rated hotels. Campton Place came under the management of the Kempinski organization, a German hotel company, in 1991. Highly attentive, personal service begins the moment uniformed doormen greet guests out-

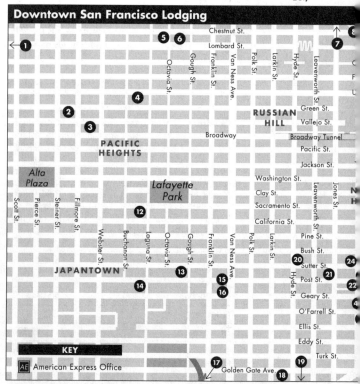

Downtown San Francisco Lodging

Abigail Hotel, **18**
Adelaide Inn, **22**
Amsterdam, **24**
Aston Pickwick Hotel, **50**
The Bed and Breakfast Inn, **4**
Beresford Arms, **21**
Best Western Americania, **51**

Campton Place Kempinski, **35**
The Cartwright, **38**
Chancellor Hotel, **39**
Columbus Motor Inn, **8**
Fairmont Hotel and Tower, **28**
Four Seasons Clift, **48**

Grand Hyatt, **36**
Grant Plaza, **34**
Handlery Hotel, **40**
Holiday Inn-Civic Center, **19**
Holiday Inn-Financial District, **30**
Hotel Britton, **52**
Hotel Diva, **45**

Huntington Hotel, **26**
Hyatt Regency, **33**
Inn at the Opera, **17**
Inn at Union Square, **44**
Kensington Park, **43**
King George, **46**
Lombard Hotel, **16**

Majestic Hotel, **13**

Mandarin Oriental, **32**

The Mansion, **12**

Marina Inn, **5**

Marina Motel, **1**

Mark Hopkins Inter-Continental, **27**

Miyako, **14**

Park Hyatt, **31**

Petite Auberge, **25**

The Prescott Hotel, **23**

Quality Hotel at Cathedral Hill, **15**

The Raphael, **47**

San Francisco Hilton on Hilton Square, **49**

San Francisco Marriott-Fisherman's Wharf, **9**

San Remo Hotel, **10**

Sheraton Palace, **41**

The Sherman House, **3**

Sir Francis Drake, **37**

Stouffer Stanford Court Hotel, **29**

Town House Motel, **6**

Tuscan Inn, **19**

Union Street Inn, **2**

Westin St. Francis, **42**

York Hotel, **20**

side the marble-floor lobby. *340 Stockton St.,
94108, tel. 415/781–5555 or 800/426–3135. 126
rooms. Facilities: restaurant, bar. AE, DC,
MC, V.*

★ **Four Seasons Clift.** Probably San Francisco's
most acclaimed hotel, this stately landmark is
the first choice of many celebrities and discrimi-
nating travelers for its attentive personal service. Special attention is given to children, with
fresh cookies and milk provided at bedtime. All
rooms are sumptuously decorated—the suites
in elegant black and gray, others in bright beige
and pink—in a somewhat updated contemporary style. *495 Geary St., 94102, tel. 415/775–
4700 or 800/332–3442. 329 rooms. Facilities: restaurant, Redwood Room lounge. AE, DC, MC,
V.*

Grand Hyatt. This hotel overlooks Union Square
and Ruth Asawa's fantasy fountain in the garden (*see* Tour 1: Union Square in Chapter 2, Exploring San Francisco). The hotel, formerly the
Hyatt on Union Square, underwent a $20 million
renovation in 1990. *345 Stockton St., 94108, tel.
415/398–1234 or 800/233–1234. 693 rooms. Facilities: 2 restaurants, 2 lounges, shopping arcade. AE, DC, MC, V.*

San Francisco Hilton on Hilton Square. A huge
expansion and renovation in 1988 made this by
far the largest hotel in San Francisco. Popular
with convention and tour groups. *1 Hilton Sq.
(O'Farrell and Mason Sts.), tel. 415/771–1400
or 800/445–8667. 1,907 rooms. Facilities: 4 restaurants, 2 lounges, pool, shopping arcade.
AE, DC, MC, V.*

Westin St. Francis. This is one of the grand hotels of San Francisco and a Union Square landmark. Rooms in the original building have been
redecorated but still retain some of the 1904
moldings and bathroom tiles. Rooms in the modern tower have brighter, lacquered furniture.
In 1991, three 40-foot tromp l'oeil murals were
installed in the renovated tower lobby, and the
main lobby received new marble floors. *335
Powell St., 94102, tel. 415/397–7000 or 800/228–
3000. 1,200 rooms. Facilities: 5 restaurants, 5
lounges, shopping arcade. AE, DC, MC, V.*

Expensive **Hotel Diva.** This hotel attracts the avant garde
set with a high-tech look that sets it apart from

any other hotel in San Francisco. *440 Geary St., 94102, tel. 415/885–0200 or 800/553–1900. 125 rooms. Facilities: restaurant, lounge. AE, DC, MC, V.*

Inn at Union Square. These individually decorated rooms with goosedown pillows and four-poster beds are sumptuous. Continental breakfast and afternoon tea are served before a fireplace in the cozy sitting areas on each floor. *440 Post St., 04102, tel. 415/397–3510 or 800/288–4346. 30 rooms. AE, DC, MC, V.*

Kensington Park. A handsome, high-ceilinged lobby sets the mood of this fine hotel, where afternoon tea and sherry are served. The rooms are decorated with English Queen Anne-style furniture. *450 Post St., 94102, tel. 415/788–6400 or 800/553–1900. 90 rooms. AE, DC, MC, V.*

★ **Petite Auberge.** The French countryside was imported to downtown San Francisco to create this charming bed-and-breakfast. Calico-printed wallpaper, fluffy down comforters, and French reproduction antiques decorate each room. Most have wood-burning fireplaces. Next door is the sister hotel, the 27-room **White Swan,** similar in style but with an English country flavor. *845 Bush St., 94108, tel. 415/928–6000. 26 rooms. Facilities: breakfast rooms, parlors. AE, MC, V.*

The Prescott Hotel. One of the plushest of the city's renovated old hotels, the Prescott may be most famous as home of Wolfgang Puck's Postrio restaurant. The hotel's emphasis is on personalized service, such as complimentary limousine service to the Financial District. *545 Post St., tel. 415/563–0303 or 800/283–7322. 167 rooms. Facilities: restaurant, lounge. AE, DC, MC, V.*

Sir Francis Drake. The rooms in this popular San Francisco hotel, famous for its Beefeater-costumed doormen, got a face-lift in 1986 during a multimillion-dollar renovation. They are decorated in an old English style, with mahogany furniture. The Starlight Roof is a lovely place for a drink. *450 Powell St., 94102, tel. 415/392–7755 or 800/227–5480. 415 rooms. Facilities: restaurant, lounge, exercise room. AE, DC, MC, V.*

Moderate **The Cartwright.** This is a family-owned hotel with a friendly, personal touch in an ideal location. Renovated in 1986 after a five-year program to instill elegance and charm into the surroundings, the property offers rooms with brass or wood-carved beds, small refrigerators, and newly tiled bathrooms. *524 Sutter St., 94102, tel. 415/421-2865 or 800/227-3844. 114 rooms. Facilities: coffee shop open for breakfast. AE, DC, MC, V.*

★ **Chancellor Hotel.** This venerable hotel has been attracting a loyal clientele since it opened in 1924. Renovated in 1986, rooms have a new, elegant appearance with polished cherry-wood furniture. One of the best buys on Union Square. *433 Powell St., 94102, tel. 415/362-2004 or 800/ 428-4748. 140 rooms. Facilities: restaurant, lounge. AE, DC, MC, V.*

Handlery Union Square Hotel. The former Handlery Motor Inn and Stewart Hotel were combined and refurbished at a cost of $5 million in early 1988. The suitelike Handlery Club rooms are larger and more expensive. *351 Geary St., 94102, tel. 415/781-7800 or 800/223-0888. 378 rooms. Facilities: restaurant, outdoor heated pool, no-smoking rooms. AE, DC, MC, V.*

Holiday Inn–Financial District. This hotel boasts an excellent location in Chinatown and is five minutes from Union Square and North Beach. Rooms on the 12th floor and above have city and bay views. *750 Kearny St., 94108, tel. 415/433-6600 or 800/465-4329. 556 rooms. Facilities: pool, restaurant, lounge. AE, DC, MC, V.*

★ **King George.** This charming midsize hotel was renovated in 1988 and 1989 to give it a more elegant, sophisticated look. The hotel's quaint Bread and Honey Tearoom serves traditional afternoon high tea. *334 Mason St., 94102, tel. 415/ 781-5050 or 800/288-6005. 144 rooms. Facilities: tearoom, lounge. AE, DC, MC, V.*

The Raphael. A favorite among repeat visitors to San Francisco, the Raphael was one of the first moderately priced European-style hotels in the city. Rooms were redecorated in 1988. The location is excellent. *386 Geary St., 94102, tel. 415/986-2000 or 800/821-5343. 151 rooms. Facilities: restaurant, lounge, in-room HBO. AE, DC, MC, V.*

York Hotel. This very attractive, renovated old

hotel is known for its Plush Room cabaret and as the site of a scene in Alfred Hitchcock's *Vertigo. 940 Sutter St., 94109, tel. 415/885–6800 or 800/227–3608. 96 rooms. Facilities: nightclub, fitness center, complimentary chauffeured limousine. AE, DC, MC, V.*

Inexpensive **Adelaide Inn.** The bedspreads may not match the drapes or carpets and the floors may creak, but the rooms are clean and cheap (less than $50 for a double room) at this friendly small hotel that is popular with Europeans. Continental breakfast is complimentary. *5 Isadora Duncan Ct. (off Taylor between Geary and Post), 94102, tel. 415/441–2474. 16 rooms, all share bath. Facilities: sitting room, refrigerator for guest use. AE, MC, V.*

Amsterdam. This European-style pension is in a Victorian building two blocks from Nob Hill. Rooms were renovated in 1988. *749 Taylor St., 94108, tel. 415/673–3277 or 800/637–3444. 30 rooms, 8 with shared bath. Facilities: cable TV in rooms, reading room, breakfast room for complimentary breakfast. AE, MC, V.*

Beresford Arms. Complimentary pastries and coffee are served in the hotel's grand old lobby. The suites with full kitchens are a good bargain for families. Standard rooms contain queen-size beds and small refrigerators. *701 Post St., 94109, tel. 415/673–2600 or 800/533–6533. 90 rooms. Facilities: some rooms have whirlpool baths. AE, DC, MC, V.*

★ **Grant Plaza.** This bargain-price hotel at the entrance of Chinatown has small but clean and attractively furnished rooms. No restaurant, but plenty of dining nearby. *465 Grant Ave., 94103, tel. 415/434–3883 or 800/472–6899. 72 rooms. AE, MC, V.*

Aston Pickwick Hotel. A renovation in 1991 dramatically upgraded the rooms in this tourist-class hotel across from the San Francisco Mint and a block from the cable car turnaround. Rooms are clean, attractively furnished, and have in-room voice mail. *85 5th St. at Mission, 94103, tel. 415/421–7500 or 800/922–7866. 189 rooms. Facilities: cocktail lounge, coffee shop, parking. AE, MC, V.*

Financial District

High-rise growth in San Francisco's Financial District has turned it into mini-Manhattan, a spectacular sight by night.

Very Expensive

Hyatt Regency. The stunning atrium-lobby architecture is the highlight here. Major renovations took place in 1990, when guest rooms were redone, and during a three-month closure of the hotel in the spring of 1993, the lobby, restaurants, and the rest of the public areas were given a warmer, more updated look. *5 Embarcadero Center, 94111, tel. 415/788-1234 or 800/233-1234. 803 rooms. Facilities: 2 restaurants, coffee shop, lounge, 24-hr room service, shopping arcade. AE, DC, MC, V.*

Mandarin Oriental. The third-highest building in San Francisco's skyline is topped by a luxurious 11-story hotel on its 38th–48th floors. It's the best for spectacular views, especially from the bathrooms in the Mandarin rooms with their floor-to-ceiling windows flanking the tubs. *222 Sansome St., 94104, tel. 415/885-0999 or 800/622-0404. 160 rooms. Facilities: gourmet restaurant, lounge. AE, DC, MC, V.*

Park Hyatt. This is the Hyatt chain's candidate for competing with the ultraluxury of some of the city's best hotels. Service is highly personal and attentive and rooms are plush, with gourmet chocolates and imported soaps. Many rooms have balconies and bay views. The hotel caters to corporate executives and the like. *333 Battery St., tel. 415/392-1234 or 800/323-7275. 360 rooms. Facilities: restaurant, lounge, library room. AE, DC, MC, V.*

Expensive

Sheraton Palace. One of the city's grand old hotels, the Sheraton reopened in 1991 after a $150 million reconstruction. New features include air-conditioning, a business center, a health club, and a pool. Happily, the Garden Court restaurant, famous for its leaded-glass ceiling, and the Pied Piper lounge, featuring Maxfield Parrish's painting of that name, were restored to their former glory. *2 New Montgomery St., 94105, tel. 415/392-8600 or 800/325-3535. 550 rooms. Facilities: 24-hr room service, 2 restaurants, 2 lounges, fitness center. AE, DC, MC, V.*

Nob Hill

Synonymous with San Francisco's high society, Nob Hill contains some of the city's best-known luxury hotels. All offer spectacular city and bay views and noted gourmet restaurants. Cable car lines that cross Nob Hill make transportation a cinch.

Very Expensive **Fairmont Hotel and Tower.** The regal "grande dame" of Nob Hill, the Fairmont has one of the most spectacular lobbies and public rooms in the city. All guest rooms are spacious and finely decorated. Those in the modern tower have the best views, while those in the old building have the stately ambience of another era. *950 Mason St., 94108, tel. 415/772–5000 or 800/527–4727. 596 rooms. Facilities: health club and spa, gift shops, 5 restaurants, 5 lounges, 24-hr room service. AE, DC, MC, V.*

★ **Huntington Hotel.** Understated class and attentive personal service are the hallmarks of this little jewel atop Nob Hill. The management is impeccably British in preserving the privacy of its celebrated guests. Each of the sumptuous rooms and suites is individually decorated, and many have splendid views of the city or the bay. *1075 California St., 94108, tel. 415/474–5400, 800/227–4683 or 800/652–1539 in CA. 143 rooms. Facilities: restaurant, lounge with entertainment. AE, DC, MC, V.*

Mark Hopkins Inter-Continental. Another Nob Hill landmark, "The Mark" is lovingly maintained. Rooms were redone in late 1987 in dramatic neoclassical furnishings of gray, silver, and khaki and with bold leaf-print bedspreads. Bathrooms are lined with Italian marble. Even-numbered rooms have views of the Golden Gate Bridge. *999 California St., 94108, tel. 415/392–3434 or 800/327–0200. 392 rooms. Facilities: gift shops, restaurant, lobby lounge, Top of the Mark cocktail lounge with panoramic views. AE, DC, MC, V.*

Stouffer Stanford Court Hotel. Since taking over three years ago, Stouffer has spent $10 million upgrading this acclaimed hotel. In 1992, a dramatic mural depicting scenes of early San Francisco was installed in the lobby under the lovely stained-glass dome. One of the city's finest restaurants, Fournou's Ovens, is here. *905 California St., 94108, tel. 415/989–3500 or 800/227–4726. 402 rooms. Facilities: gift shops, 2 restaurants, 2 lounges. AE, DC, MC, V.*

Fisherman's Wharf/North Beach

Fisherman's Wharf, San Francisco's top tourist attraction, is also the most popular area for accommodations. All are within a couple of blocks of restaurants, shops, and cable car lines. Because of city ordinances, none of the hotels exceed four stories; thus, this is not the area for fantastic views of the city or bay. Reservations are always necessary, sometimes weeks in advance during the peak summer months (when hotel rates rise by as much as 30%). Some streetside rooms can be noisy.

Very Expensive   **San Francisco Marriott–Fisherman's Wharf.** Elegant lobby and guest rooms set the mood in one of the wharf's newest and finest hotels. *1250 Columbus Ave., 94133, tel. 415/775–7555 or 800/228–9290. 256 rooms. Facilities: restaurant, lounge, gift shop. AE, DC, MC, V.*

Expensive   **Tuscan Inn.** One of the newest hotels at the wharf, this hotel has an Italian flavor, as its name implies. Room service is provided by Cafe Pescatore, the hotel restaurant, which specializes in Italian seafood dishes. *425 Northpoint St., 94133, tel. 415/561–1100 or 800/648–4626. 220 rooms. Facilities: valet parking, 24-hr complimentary coffee and tea, morning limousine to Financial District, no-smoking rooms. AE, DC, MC, V.*

Moderate   **Columbus Motor Inn.** This is an attractive motel between the wharf and North Beach with suites that are ideal for families. *1075 Columbus Ave., 94133, tel. 415/885–1492. 45 rooms. Facilities: free parking. AE, DC, MC, V.*

Inexpensive ★   **San Remo Hotel.** This cozy hotel is reminiscent of a European-style pension. Renovated during recent years, its smallish rooms and narrow corridors are freshly painted and decorated with plants and antiques. It offers a good location on the border of Fisherman's Wharf and North Beach. *2237 Mason St., 94133, tel. 415/776–8688. 62 rooms, all with shared baths. Daily and* *weekly rates. Facilities: restaurant. AE, DC, MC, V.*

Lombard Street/Cow Hollow

Lombard Street, a major traffic corridor leading to the Golden Gate Bridge, is sandwiched between two of San Francisco's poshest neighborhoods, Cow Hollow and the Marina District.

Very Expensive ★ **The Sherman House.** In the middle of an elegant residential district is this magnificent landmark mansion, the most luxurious small hotel in San Francisco. Each room is individually decorated with Biedermeier, English Jacobean, or French Second-Empire antiques, with tapestrylike canopies covering four-poster beds. Marble-top, wood-burning fireplaces, and black granite bathrooms with whirlpool baths complete the picture. There is an in-house restaurant for guests only. *2160 Green St., 94123, tel. 415/563–3600. 15 rooms. Facilities: dining room, sitting rooms. AE, DC, MC, V.*

Moderate **The Bed and Breakfast Inn.** The first of San Francisco's B&Bs, this is an ivy-covered renovated Victorian in an alleyway off Union Street. Romantic, cheery rooms with flowery wallpaper include "The Mayfair," a flat with a spiral staircase leading to a sleeping loft. Some rooms are more modest and share baths. *4 Charlton Ct., 94123, tel. 415/921–9784. 11 rooms with baths. Facilities: breakfast room. No credit cards.*

★ **Marina Inn.** Here cute B&B-style accommodations are offered at motel prices. Dainty-flowered wallpaper, poster beds, country pine furniture, and fresh flowers give the rooms an English country air. Continental breakfast is served in the cozy central sitting room. Turned-down beds and chocolates greet guests at the end of the day. No parking. *3110 Octavia St. at Lombard St., 94123, tel. 415/928–1000. 40 rooms. Facilities: lounge. AE, MC, V.*

Union Street Inn. A retired schoolteacher has transformed this 1902 Edwardian home into a cozy inn. Antiques and fresh flowers are found throughout. *2229 Union St., 94123, tel. 415/346–0424. 6 rooms with private bath. Facilities: English garden, breakfast room. AE, MC, V.*

Inexpensive **Marina Motel.** This quaint Spanish-style stucco complex is one of the oldest motels on Lombard Street, but it is well kept. Each room has its own garage. *2576 Lombard St., 94123, tel. 415/921–9406. 45 rooms, some with kitchen. Facilities: free parking. AE, MC, V.*

★ **Town House Motel.** A very attractive motel with recently redecorated rooms, this is one of the best values on Lombard Street. *1650 Lombard St., 94123, tel. 415/885–5163 or 800/255–1516. 24 rooms. Facilities: free parking. AE, DC, MC, V.*

Civic Center/Van Ness

The governmental heart of San Francisco has been undergoing a renaissance that has made it come alive with fine restaurants, trendy night spots, and renovated small hotels.

Expensive **Quality Hotel at Cathedral Hill.** All the guest rooms were renovated in 1988 at this popular convention hotel. *1101 Van Ness Ave., 94109, tel. 415/776–8200, 800/227–4730, or 800/622–0855 in CA. 400 rooms. Facilities: free parking, pool, 2 restaurants, lounge. AE, DC, MC, V.*

★ **Inn at the Opera.** A music or ballet lover's heart may quiver at the sight of this lovely small hotel, where musicians and singers stay when they appear at San Francisco's performing arts centers a block away. There are billowing pillows, terry-cloth robes, microwave ovens, and servibars in each room. *333 Fulton St., 94102, tel. 415/863–8400, 800/325–2708, or 800/423–9610 in CA. 48 rooms. Facilities: restaurant, lounge. AE, DC, MC, V.*

Miyako. In the heart of Japantown is this elegant, recently renovated hotel. The Japanese ambience is established by a greeting from a kimono-clad hostess. Traditional Japanese rooms with tatami mats are available. *1625 Post St., at Laguna St., 94115, tel. 415/922–3200 or 800/533–4567. 218 rooms. Facilities: Japanese baths, saunas, restaurant, 2 lounges. AE, DC, MC, V.*

Moderate **Abigail Hotel.** A former B&B inn, this hotel re-
★ tains its homey atmosphere with an eclectic mix of English antiques and mounted hunting trophies in the lobby. Hissing steam radiators and

sleigh beds set the mood in the antiques-filled rooms. Room 211—the hotel's only suite—is the most elegant and spacious. *246 McAllister St., 94102, tel. 415/861-9728 or 800/243-6510. 62 rooms. AE, DC, MC, V.*

Best Western Americania. Distinguished by its pink-and-turquoise Moorish facade, this Best Western has quiet rooms that overlook inner courtyards with fountain or swimming pool. *121 7th St., 94103, tel. 415/626-0200 or 800/444-5816. 142 rooms. Facilities: outdoor pool, sauna, coffee shop, free parking, no-smoking rooms available, evening shuttle to Union Sq. AE, DC, MC, V.*

Holiday Inn-Civic Center. A 1989 renovation of the exterior, all rooms, lobby, and the restaurant has added a touch of elegance to this chain hotel. The location is good—three blocks from the Civic Center and two blocks from Brooks Hall/Civic Auditorium. *50 8th St., 94103, tel. 415/626-6103 or 800/465-4329. 390 rooms. Facilities: restaurant, lounge, outdoor pool. AE, DC, MC, V.*

★ **Lombard Hotel.** This is a European-style hotel with a handsome marble-floor lobby flanked on one side by the Gray Derby restaurant. Many of the rooms were refurbished in 1989 with bland-wood furniture and new servibars. Quiet rooms are in the back. Complimentary evening cocktails and chauffeured limousine downtown are offered. *1015 Geary St., 94109, tel. 415/673-5232 or 800/227-3608. 100 rooms. Facilities: restaurant. AE, DC, MC, V.*

Majestic Hotel. One of San Francisco's original grand hotels, the Majestic was meticulously restored and reopened in 1985 with even more stately elegance. Romantic rooms have French and English antiques and four-poster canopy beds. Many have fireplaces and original claw-foot bathtubs. *1500 Sutter St., 94109, tel. 415/441-1100 or 800/869-8966. 60 rooms. Facilities: gourmet restaurant, lounge. AE, DC, MC, V.*

The Mansion. This twin-turreted Queen Anne was built in 1887 and today houses one of the most unusual hotels in the city. Rooms contain an oddball collection of furnishings and vary from the tiny "Tom Thumb" room to the opulent "Josephine" suite, the favorite of such celebrities as Barbra Streisand. Owner Bob Pritikin's pig paintings and other "porkabilia" are every-where. Full breakfast is included. *2220 Sacramento St., 94115, tel. 415/929-9444. 28 rooms. Facilities: dining room, weekend concerts, sculpture and flower garden. AE, DC, MC, V.*

Inexpensive **Hotel Britton.** This hotel is clean and comfort-
★ able, with good rates, and is near the Civic Cen-ter. Rooms are attractively furnished, and color TVs offer in-room movies. *112 7th St., at Mission St., 94103, tel. 415/621-7001 or 800/444-5819. 80 rooms. Facilities: coffee shop. AE, DC, MC, V.*

6 The Arts and Nightlife

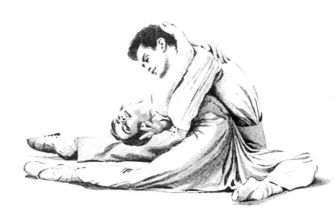

The Arts

By Robert
Taylor

Robert Taylor
is a longtime
San
Francisco
arts and
entertainment
writer.

The best guide to arts and entertainment events
in San Francisco is the "Datebook" section,
printed on pink paper, in the Sunday *Examiner
and Chronicle*. The *Bay Guardian* and *S.F.
Weekly*, free and available in racks around the
city, list more neighborhood, avant-garde, and
budget-priced events. For up-to-date information about cultural and musical events, call the
Convention and Visitors Bureau's *Cultural
Events Calendar* (tel. 415/391–2001).

Half-price tickets to many local and touring
stage shows go on sale (cash only) at 11 AM.
Tuesday–Saturday at the TIX Bay Area booth
on the Stockton Street side of Union Square, between Geary and Post streets. TIX is also a full-
service ticket agency for theater and music
events around the Bay Area (open until 6 PM
Tuesday–Thursday, 7 PM Friday–Saturday).
While the city's major commercial theaters are
concentrated downtown, the opera, symphony,
and ballet perform at the Civic Center. For recorded information about TIX tickets, call 415/
433–7827.

The city's charge-by-phone ticket service is
BASS (tel. 510/762–2277), with one of its centers
in the STBS booth mentioned above and another
at **Tower Records** (Bay St. at Columbus Ave.),
near Fisherman's Wharf. Other agencies downtown are the **City Box Office**, 141 Kearny Street
in the Sherman Clay store (tel. 415/392–4400)
and **Downtown Center Box Office** in the parking
garage at 320 Mason Street (tel. 415/775–2021).
The opera, symphony, the ballet's *Nutcracker*,
and touring hit musicals are often sold out in advance; tickets are usually available within a day
of performance for other shows.

Theater

San Francisco's "theater row" is a single block of
Geary Street west of Union Square, but a number of commercial theaters are located within
walking distance, along with resident companies that enrich the city's theatrical scene. The
three major commercial theaters are operated

by the Shorenstein-Nederlander organization, which books touring plays and musicals, some of them before they open on Broadway. The most venerable is the **Curran** (445 Geary St., tel. 415/474–3800), which is used for plays and smaller musicals. The **Golden Gate** is a stylishly refurbished movie theater (Golden Gate Ave. at Taylor St., tel. 415/474–3800), primarily a musical house. The 2,500-seat **Orpheum** (1192 Market St. near the Civic Center, tel. 415/474–3800) is used for the biggest touring shows.

The smaller commercial theaters, offering touring shows and a few that are locally produced, are the **Marines Memorial Theatre** (Sutter and Mason Sts., tel. 415/441–7444) and **Theatre on the Square** (450 Post St., tel. 415/433–9500). For commercial and popular success, nothing beats *Beach Blanket Babylon*, the zany revue that has been running for years at **Club Fugazi** (678 Green St. in North Beach, tel. 415/421–4222). Conceived by imaginative San Francisco director Steve Silver, it is a lively, colorful musical mix of cabaret, show-biz parodies, and tributes to local landmarks. *(See* Cabarets in Nightlife, *below.)*

The city's major theater company is the **American Conservatory Theatre (ACT),** which quickly became one of the nation's leading regional theaters when it was founded during the mid-1960s. It presents a season of approximately eight plays in rotating repertory from October through late spring. The ACT's ticket office is at the **Geary Theatre** (415 Geary St., tel. 415/749–2228), though the theater itself was closed following the 1989 earthquake. During reconstruction ACT is performing at the nearby **Stage Door Theater** (420 Mason St.) and the **Theatre on the Square** (450 Post St.).

The leading producer of new plays is the **Magic Theatre** (Bldg. D, Fort Mason Center, Laguna St. at Marina Blvd., tel. 415/441–8822). The city boasts a wide variety of specialized and ethnic theaters that work with dedicated local actors and some professionals. Among the most interesting are **The Lamplighters,** the delightful Gilbert and Sullivan troupe that often gets better reviews than touring productions of musicals, performing at **Presentation Theater** (2350 Turk St., tel. 415/752–7755); the **Lorraine Hansberry Theatre,** which specializes in plays by black writers (620 Sutter St., tel. 415/474–8800); the **Asian American Theatre** (405 Arguello Blvd., tel. 415/346–8922); and two stages that showcase gay and lesbian performers; **Theatre Rhinoceros** (2926 16th St., tel. 415/861–5079) and **Josie's Cabaret and Juice Joint** (3583 16th St., tel. 415/861–7933). The **San Francisco Shakespeare Festival** offers free performances on summer weekends in Golden Gate Park (tel. 415/221–0642).

Avant-garde theater, dance, opera, and "performance art" turn up in a variety of locations, not all of them theaters. The major presenting organization is the **Theater Artaud** (499 Alabama St. in the Mission District, tel. 415/621–7797), which is situated in a huge, converted machine shop. One more trendy performance center is the **Climate** theater (252 9th St., tel. 415/626–9196), in the neighborhood of the newest cafés, clubs, and galleries.

Music

The completion of Davies Symphony Hall at Van Ness Avenue and Grove Street finally gave the San Francisco Symphony a home of its own. It solidified the base of the city's three major performing arts organizations—symphony, opera, and ballet—in the Civic Center. The symphony and other musical groups also perform in the smaller, 928-seat Herbst Theatre in the Opera's "twin" at Van Ness Avenue and McAllister Street, the War Memorial Building. Otherwise the city's musical ensembles can be found all over the map: in churches and museums, in restaurants and outdoors in parks, and in outreach series in Berkeley and on the peninsula.

San Francisco Symphony (Davies Symphony Hall, Van Ness Ave. at Grove St., tel. 510/431–5400. Tickets at the box office or through BASS, tel. 415/762–2277). The city's most stable performing arts organization plays from September through May, with music director Herbert

Blomstedt conducting for about two-thirds of the season. Guest conductors often include Michael Tilson Thomas, Edo de Waart, and Riccardo Muti. Guest soloists include artists of the caliber of Andre Watts, Peter Serkin, and Pinchas Zukerman. Special events include a Mostly Mozart festival during the spring, a Beethoven festival during the summer, a "Wet Ink" festival of new music during the spring in the more intimate Herbst Theatre, and summer Pops Concerts in the nearby Civic Auditorium. Throughout the season, the symphony presents a Great Performers Series of guest soloists and orchestras.

Philharmonia Baroque (Herbst Theatre, Van Ness Ave. at McAllister St., tel. 415/552–3656. Tickets also at STBS booth in Union Square). This stylish ensemble has been called the local baroque orchestra with the national reputation. Its season of concerts, fall-spring, celebrates composers of the 17th and 18th centuries, including Handel, Vivaldi, and Mozart.

San Francisco Chamber Symphony (various locations, tel. 415/441–4636). Under artistic advisor Donald Runnicles, this group has become known for the variety of its programming, which can include composers from Handel to Villa-Lobos.

Kronos Quartet (Herbst Theatre and other locations, tel. 415/731–3533). Twentieth-century works and a number of premiers make up the programs for this group that goes as far as possible to prove that string quartets are not stodgy.

Midsummer Mozart (Herbst Theatre and occasionally at Davies Symphony Hall, tel. 415/781–5931). This is one of the few Mozart festivals that hasn't filled programs with works by other composers. It performs in July and August under George Cleve, conductor of the San Jose Symphony.

Old First Concerts (Old First Church, Van Ness Ave. at Sacramento St., tel. 415/474–1608. Tickets also at STBS booth, Union Square). This is a well-respected Friday evening and Sunday afternoon series of chamber music, vocal soloists, new music, and jazz.

Pops Concerts (Polk and Grove Sts., tel. 415/431–5400). Many members of the symphony per-

form in the July pops series in the 7,000-seat
Civic Auditorium. The schedule includes light
classics, Broadway, country, and movie music.
Tickets cost as little as a few dollars.

Stern Grove (Sloat Blvd. at 19th Ave., tel. 415/
252–6252). This is the nation's oldest continual
free summer music festival, offering 10 Sunday
afternoons of symphony, opera, jazz, pop music,
and dance. The amphitheater is in a eucalyptus
grove below street level; remember that summer in this area near the ocean can be cool.

There are also free band concerts on Sunday and
holiday afternoons in the Golden Gate Park music concourse (tel. 415/558–3706) opposite the de
Young Museum.

Opera

San Francisco Opera (Van Ness Ave. at Grove
St., tel. 415/864–3330). Founded in 1923, and
the resident company at the War Memorial Opera House in the Civic Center since it was built
in 1932, the Opera has expanded to a fall season
of 13 weeks. Approximately 70 performances of
10 operas are given, beginning on the first Friday after Labor Day. For many years the Opera
was considered a major international company
and the most artistically successful operatic organization in the United States. International
competition and management changes have
made recent seasons uneven; the company has
revitalized under general director Lotfi
Mansouri, formerly head of Toronto's Canadian
Opera Company. International opera stars frequently sing major roles here, but the Opera is
also well known for presenting the American de-
buts of singers who have made their name in Europe. In the same way, the company's standard
repertoire is interspersed with revivals of rarely heard works.

The Opera was one of the first to present
"supertitles," English translations projected
above the stage during performances. The system is used for almost all operas not sung in English. In addition to the fall season, the Opera
performs Wagner's Ring cycle every five sum-
mers—next in 1995. Ticket prices range from
about $28 to a high of about $90, and many per-

formances are sold out far in advance. Standing-room tickets are always sold, however, and patrons often sell extra tickets on the Opera House steps just before curtain time.

Pocket Opera (tel. 415/989–1853). This lively, modestly priced alternative to "grand" opera gives concert performances, mostly in English, of rarely heard works. Offenbach's operettas are frequently on the bill during the winter-spring season. Concerts are held at various locations.

Another operatic alternative is the **Lamplighters** *(see* Theater, *above)*, which specializes in Gilbert and Sullivan but presents other light operas as well.

Dance

San Francisco Ballet (War Memorial Opera House, Van Ness Ave. at Grove St., tel. 415/703–9400). The ballet has regained much of its luster under artistic director Helgi Tomasson, and both classical and contemporary works have won admiring reviews. The company's primary season runs February–May; its repertoire includes such full-length ballets as *Swan Lake* and a new production of *Sleeping Beauty*. The company is also intent on reaching new audiences with bold new dances, what it likes to call "cutting-edge works that will make you take a second look." Like many dance companies in the nation, the ballet presents *The Nutcracker* in December, and its recent production is one of the most spectacular.

Margaret Jenkins Dance Company (Theater Artaud, 450 Florida St., tel. 415/863–1173). This is one of the most reliable of the city's modern experimental dance troupes, in which the dancers themselves help shape the choreography.

Ethnic Dance Festival (Palace of Fine Arts Theatre, Bay and Lyon Sts., tel. 415/474–3914). Approximately 30 of the Bay Area's estimated 200 ethnic dance companies and soloists perform on several programs in June. Prices are modest for the city-sponsored event.

San Francisco and the Bay Area support innumerable experimental and ethnic dance groups.

Among them are ODC/San Francisco (tel. 415/ 863–6606), performing at Herbst Theatre (Van Ness Ave.); the **Joe Goode Performance Group** (tel. 415/648–4848); and **Rosa Montoya Bailes Flamenco** (tel. 415/931–7374), which often performs at Herbst Theatre. The **Footworks Studio** (3221 22nd St., tel. 415/824–5044) gives many more local dancers a chance to perform.

Film

The San Francisco Bay Area, including Berkeley and San Jose, is considered one of the nation's most important movie markets. If there is a film floating around the country or around the world in search of an audience, it is likely that it will eventually turn up on a screen in San Francisco. The Bay Area is also a film-making center: Documentaries and experimental works are being produced on modest budgets, feature films and television programs are shot on location, and some of Hollywood's biggest directors prefer to live here, particularly in Marin County. In San Francisco, about a third of the theaters regularly show foreign and independent films. The city is also one of the last strongholds of "repertory cinema," showing older American and foreign films on bills that change daily.

San Francisco's traditional movie theater center, downtown on Market Street, is pretty much given over to sex and action movies nowadays. First-run commercial movie theaters are now scattered throughout the city, although they are concentrated along Van Ness Avenue, near Japantown, and in the Marina District. All are accessible on major Muni bus routes, as are the art-revival houses. Several of the most respected and popular independent theaters have been taken over by chains recently, and their policy could change. The San Francisco International Film Festival *(see below)*, the oldest in the country, continues to provide an extensive selection of foreign films each spring.

Foreign and Independent Films The most reliable theaters for foreign and independent films are **Opera Plaza Cinemas** (Van Ness Ave. at Golden Gate Ave., tel. 415/771– 0102); **Lumiere** (California St. near Polk St., tel. 415/885–3200); **Clay** (Fillmore and Clay Sts., tel. 415/346–1123); **Gateway** (215 Jackson St. at Battery St., tel. 415/421–3353); **Castro** (Castro St. near Market St., tel. 415/621–6120), the last remaining movie palace from the 1920s that is still showing movies, with an extensive schedule of revivals; and **Bridge** (3013 Geary Blvd. near Masonic Ave., tel. 415/751–3212).

Festivals **The San Francisco International Film Festival** (tel. 415/931–3456) takes over several theaters for two weeks in late April at the AMC Kabuki complex at Post and Fillmore streets. The festival schedules about 75 films from abroad, many of them American premieres, along with a variety of independent American documentaries. During recent years there has been an emphasis on films from Africa and Asia.

Other showcases for films out of the commercial mainstream include the **Roxie Cinema** (3116 16th St., tel. 415/863–1087), which specializes in social and political documentaries; the **Cinematheque** at the San Francisco Art Institute (800 Chestnut St., tel. 415/558–8129), which often features films and personal appearances by avant-garde artists; and **Eye Gallery** (1151 Mission St., tel. 415/431–6911), which offers experimental videos and films.

Nightlife

By Daniel Mangin

A longtime Bay Area resident, Daniel Mangin writes on the arts for several local papers. He is an instructor of film history at City College of San Francisco.

San Francisco provides a tremendous potpourri of evening entertainment ranging from ultrasophisticated cabarets to bawdy bistros that reflect the city's gold-rush past. With the exception of the hotel lounges and discos noted below, the accent is on casual dress—call ahead if you are uncertain.

For information on who is performing where, check the following sources: The Sunday San Francisco *Examiner and Chronicle*'s pink "Datebook" insert lists major events and cultural happenings. The free alternative weeklies, the *Bay Guardian* and *SF Weekly*, are terrific sources for current music clubs and comedy. Another handy reference for San Francisco nightlife is *Key* magazine, offered free in most major hotel lobbies. For a phone update on sports and musical events, call the Convention and Visitor Bureau's *Events Hotline* (tel. 415/391–2001). Those seeking weekly jazz headliners should dial the KJAZ *Jazz Line* (tel. 510/769–4818).

Although San Francisco is a compact city with the prevailing influences of some neighborhoods spilling into others, the following generalizations should help you find the kind of entertainment you're looking for. **Nob Hill** is noted for its plush piano bars and panoramic skyline lounges. **North Beach,** infamous for its topless and bottomless bistros, also maintains a sense of its beatnik past and this legacy lives on in atmospheric bars and coffeehouses. **Fisherman's Wharf,** while touristy, is great for people watching and provides plenty of impromptu entertainment from street performers. **Union Street** is home away from home for singles in search of company. South of Market (SoMa, for short) has become a hub of nightlife, with a bevy of highly popular nightclubs, bars, and lounges in renovated warehouses and auto shops. Gay men will find the **Castro** and **Polk Street** scenes of infinite variety.

Rock, Pop, Folk, and Blues

The hip SoMa scene of a few years ago has mellowed a bit of late; the clubs still feature fine music, but the trendoids have bailed out. Musical offerings in this part of town and elsewhere run from mainstream to way, way out.

Bottom of the Hill. This great little club "two minutes south of SoMa" in the Potrero Hill District showcases some of the best local alternative rock and blues in the city. The atmosphere is ultra low-key, though even these cool folks start a-buzzin' when the occasional rock or pop star drops in to check out the scene. *1233 17th St. at Texas St., tel. 415/626-4455. Shows begin 9:30–10 PM. Cover $3–$7.*

DNA Lounge. Alternative independent rock, funk, and rap are the usual fare at this hip but friendly venue. *375 11th St. near Harrison St., tel. 415/626–1409. Live bands most nights at 10 PM. Other nights the club is open for dancing to*

recorded music. Cover: Varies weeknights from
none to $5, Fri.–Sat. $7. No credit cards.

Freight and Salvage Coffee House. This is one of
the finest folk houses in the country; it's worth a
trip across the bay. Some of the most talented
practitioners of folk, blues, Cajun, and blue-
grass perform at the Freight, among them U.
Utah Phillips and Rosalie Sorrels. 1111 Addison
St., Berkeley, tel. 510/548–1761. Shows: Sun.
and Tues. Thurs. 8 PM, Fri. and Sat. 8:30. Cover: $6–$12. No credit cards.

Great American Music Hall. This is one of the
great eclectic nightclubs, not only in San Francisco but in the entire country. Here you will
find truly top-drawer entertainment, running
the gamut from the best in blues, folk, and jazz
to rock with a sprinkling of outstanding comedians. This colorful marble-pillared emporium
will also accommodate dancing to popular
bands. Past headliners here include Carmen
McCrae, B.B. King, Billy Bragg, NRBQ, and
Doc Watson. 859 O'Farrell St. between Polk and
Larkin Sts., tel. 415/885–0750. Shows usually
at 8 PM, but this may vary, so call. Cover: $5–
$20. No credit cards.

Jack's Bar. This smoky R&B dive has been serving up hot music since 1932. There's dancing
seven nights a week in a soulful atmosphere.
The club's jam sessions are legendary. It's best
to take a cab to and from this place. 1601 Fillmore St., tel. 415/567–3227. Shows begin at 9
PM. No cover Sun.–Thurs., $5 Fri. and Sat.
nights. No credit cards.

Last Day Saloon. In an attractive setting of
wooden tables and potted plants, this club offers
some major entertainers and a varied schedule
of blues, Cajun, rock, and jazz. Some of the illus-
trious performers who have appeared here are
Taj Mahal, the Zazu Pitts Memorial Orchestra,
Maria Muldaur, and Pride and Joy. 406 Clement
St., between 5th and 6th Aves. in the Richmond
District, tel. 415/387–6343. Shows 9 PM nightly.
Cover: $4–$20. No credit cards.

The Saloon. Some locals consider the historic
Saloon the best spot in San Francisco for the
blues. Headliners here include local R&B favorites Johnny Nitro and the Doorslammers. 1232
Grant St., near Columbus Ave. in North Beach,

tel. 415/989–7666. Shows 9:30 PM nightly. Cover: $5–$8 Fri. and Sat. No credit cards.

Slim's. One of the most popular nightclubs on the SoMa scene, Slim's specializes in what it labels "American roots music"—blues, jazz, classic rock, and the like. The club has expanded its repertoire in recent years with national touring acts playing alternative rock-and-roll and a series of "spoken word" concerts. Co-owner Boz Scaggs helps bring in the crowds and famous headliners. *333 11th St., tel. 415/621–3330. Shows nightly 9 PM. Cover: none–$20, depending on the night and act. AE, MC, V.*

The Warfield. This old movie palace was completely renovated in 1988 to become a showcase for mainstream rock-and-roll. There are tables and chairs downstairs, and theater seating upstairs. Such contemporary acts as the Jerry Garcia Band, Sonic Youth, and k.d. lang have played here recently. *982 Market St. tel. 415/ 775–7722. Shows most nights at 8 PM. Tickets $15–$30. No credit cards (except through the BASS ticket agency).*

Jazz

The jazz scene in San Francisco has been heating up of late. Your options run the gamut from a mellow restaurant cocktail lounge to hip SoMa venues to stylish showcases for top acts.

Cafe du Nord. What was once a Basque restaurant now hosts some of the liveliest jam sessions in town. The atmosphere in this basement poolroom/bar is decidedly casual, but the music, provided mostly by local talent, is strictly top-notch. *2170 Market St. at Sanchez, tel. 415/861– 5016. Open daily 4 PM–2 AM, with live music 7 nights a week, beginning at 9. Cover: $2, no drink minimum.*

Jazz at Pearl's. This club is one of the few reminders of North Beach's days as a hot spot for cool tunes. Sophisticated and romantic, the club's picture windows overlook City Lights Bookstore across the street. The talent level is remarkably high, especially considering that there is often no cover weeknights (and even some weekends). *256 Columbus Ave., near Broadway, tel. 415/291–8255. Live music nightly, beginning at 9–9:30 PM. Cover: none most* *weekdays, none–$5 weekends, 2-drink minimum every night.*

Kimball's. This attractive, brick-walled Civic Center nightclub and restaurant books top national jazz names such as Mose Allison, Cedar Walton, and Ahmad Jamal. *300 Grove St., tel. 415/861–5555. Live music Wed.–Sat. at 9 and 11 PM, Sun. 8 and 10 PM. Cover: $12–$15 with $5 minimum food or drink order per person. AE, MC, V.*

Moose's. One of the city's hottest new restaurants also features great sounds in its smallish but stylish bar area. *1652 Stockton St., in North Beach, tel. 415/989–7800. First set begins after 8 PM; music continues until midnight. No cover.*

Up and Down Club. This hip restaurant and club, formerly Eddie Jack's, often books up-and-coming jazz artists in its downstairs bar. There's dancing some nights. Upstairs at the Tap Room bar, live jazz alternates with recorded music. *1151 Folsom St., tel. 415/626–2388. Shows begin at 8 PM. No cover most nights.*

Cabarets

Traditional cabaret is in short supply in San Francisco, but two long-time favorite spots and a couple of alternative venues offer a range of entertainment.

Club Fugazi. *Beach Blanket Babylon* is a wacky musical revue that has become the longest-running show of its genre in the history of the theater. It has been playing now for two decades, outstripping the Ziegfeld Follies by years. While the choreography is colorful and the songs witty, the real stars of the show are the exotic costumes—worth the price of admission in themselves. Order tickets as far in advance as possible; the revue has been sold out up to a month in advance. *678 Green St., 94133, tel. 415/421–4222 (for an order form, fax 415/421–4817). Shows Wed. and Thurs. 7 PM, Fri. and Sat. 7 and 10 PM, Sun. 3 and 7 PM. Cover: $17–$40, depending upon date and seating location. Note: those under 21 are admitted only to the Sun. matinee performance. MC, V.*

Finocchio's. The female impersonators at this amiable, world-famous club have been generating confusion for 56 years now. The scene at

Finocchio's is decidedly retro, which for the most part only adds to its charm. *506 Broadway, North Beach, tel. 415/982–9388. Note: those under 21 not admitted. Shows Tues. and Thurs.– Sun. nightly at 8:30, 10, and 11:30 (closed Sun. and Tues. in the off-season). Cover: $15, no drink minimum. MC, V.*

Comedy Clubs

Holy City Zoo. Robin Williams ascended like a meteor from an improv group that gained fame here, and terrific standup comics headline now. The "Zoo" features an open mike for pros and would-be comedians every Tuesday. Call ahead; rumor has it the club may close. *408 Clement St. in the Richmond District, tel. 415/386–4242. Shows Sun.–Thurs. 9 PM, Fri.–Sat. 9 and 11 PM. Cover: $3 Sun.–Thurs., $8 Fri. and Sat., 2-drink minimum. MC, V.*

The Improv Comedy Club. National and up-and-coming stand-up comics hold court at this Union Square-area venue. On Monday nights, local improv group the National Theatre of Deranged lives up to its name. *401 Mason St., at Geary St., tel. 415/441–7787. Shows Mon. 8 PM, Tues.– Thurs. and Sun. 9 PM, Fri. and Sat. 9 and 11 PM. Cover: $8 weeknights, $10 weekends and 2-drink minimum. MC, V.*

The Punch Line. A launching pad for the likes of Jay Leno and Whoopie Goldberg, the Punch Line features some of the top talents around— several of whom are certain to make a national impact. Note that weekend shows often sell out, and it is best to buy tickets in advance at BASS outlets (tel. 415/762–BASS). *444-A Battery St. between Clay and Washington Sts., tel. 415/ 397–PLSF. Shows Sun.–Thurs. 9 PM, Fri. 9 and 11 PM, Sat. 7, 9, and 11:30 PM. Cover: $8 Tues.–Thurs.; $10 Fri. and Sat.; special $5 showcases Mon. and Sun. 2-drink minimum. MC, V.*

Dancing Emporiums

Some of the rock, blues, and jazz clubs listed above sport active dance floors. Some also feature DJ dancing when live acts aren't on the stage. Below are seven spots devoted solely to folks out to shake a tail feather.

Bahia Tropical. Here's a truly international club. Dance to Salsa, Caribbean, African, Latin, and Brazilian music (sometimes on the same night) at this always-jumping joint. Cover includes dance lessons (Salsa on Thursday, Brazilian on Saturday) some nights. The crowd is young and casual. Live music Thursday–Saturday, and occasionally other evenings. *1600 Market St., tel. 415/861–8657 Dancing begins 9–9:30 Mon.–Sat., 5 PM on Sun., and lasts until 1:30 AM. Cover: $5–$10.*

Bridge. This site with a stage for live acts and a large dance floor has housed a number of clubs over the years. Underground chic ('90s style) rules here now: the Wednesday "Bondage A Go-Go" features grunge music and body piercings; the rest of the week is alternately live and recorded industrial/subpop music. Call ahead; Bridge may be closing. *520 4th St. at Bryant. Shows Wed.–Sun. at 9 PM. Cover: none–$8. No credit cards.*

Cesar's Latin Palace. Salsa-style Latin music attracts all kinds of dancers to this popular club in the city's Hispanic Mission District. Latin dance lessons from 9 to 10 PM are included in the price of admission Friday and Saturday nights. Note: no alcohol is served here. *3140 Mission St., tel. 415/648–6611. Open Sun. and Thurs. 8 PM–2 AM, Fri. and Sat. 9 PM–5 AM. Cover: $5–$7, which includes nearby parking and coat check.*

Club DV8. One of the largest of the trendy SoMa clubs, DV8 attracts scores of stylish young people to its 25,000 square feet (two levels) of dance floors. *540 Howard St., tel. 415/957–1730. Open Wed.–Sat. 9 PM–3 AM. Cover: $5–$10.*

Club O. This dance spot gets its name from the swimming pool adjacent. It was the original SoMa crossover bar; ironically, it's now gay again one night (Thursday) a week. The cover charge varies. Note: You must be 21 to enter. *278 11th St., South of Market, tel. 415/621–8119. Opens 9:30 PM.*

The Kennel Club. Alternative rock and funk rule in this small, steamy room: Everyone's dancing! On Thursdays this space is known as The Box, and a very gay mixed-gender, mixed-race crowd takes over. On weekends, DJs spin worldbeat and reggae, unless a live act (such as Zulu Spear or Sister Double Happiness) has been booked. *628 Divisadero, tel. 415/931–1914. Open nightly 9 PM–2 AM. Cover: $3–$10.*

Oz. The most popular upscale disco in San Francisco, the land of Oz is reached via a glass elevator. Then, surrounded by a splendid panorama of the city, you dance on marble floors and recharge on cushy sofas and bamboo chairs. The fine sound system belts out oldies, disco, Motown, and new wave. *335 Powell St. between Geary and Post Sts. on the top floor of the Westin St. Francis Hotel, tel. 415/397–7000. Open Sun.–Thurs. 9 PM–1:30 AM, Fri. and Sat. 9–2:30. Cover: $8 Sun.–Thurs.; $15 Fri.–Sat.*

Piano Bars

You only have eyes for her. Or him. Six quiet spots with talented tinklers provide the perfect atmosphere for holding hands, making plans.

Act IV Lounge. A popular spot for a romantic rendezvous, the focal point of this elegant lounge is a crackling fireplace. *At the Inn at the Opera, 333 Fulton St. near Franklin St., tel. 415/553–8100. Pianist nightly 6–9. No cover.*

Masons. The talented Peter Mintun plays pop and show standards at this elegant restaurant in the Fairmont Hotel. *California and Mason Sts., tel. 415/392–0113. Wed.–Thurs. 6–11, Fri. and Sat. 7–midnight. No cover. Dress: elegant.*

Ritz-Carlton Hotel. The tastefully appointed Lobby Lounge features a harpist for high tea daily from 2:30 to 5:30 PM. Afternoon tea here is perhaps the best in town. The lounge shifts to piano (with occasional vocal accompaniment) for cocktails until 11:30 each night. *600 Stockton St., tel. 415/296–7465.*

Washington Square Bar and Grill. A favorite of San Francisco politicians and newspapermen, the "Washbag," as it is affectionately known, hosts pianists performing jazz and popular standards. *On North Beach's Washington Sq., 1707 Powell St., tel. 415/982–8123. Music Mon.–Sat. from 9 PM. No cover.*

Skyline Bars

San Francisco is a city of spectacular vistas. Enjoy drinks, music, and sometimes dinner with 360-degree views at any of the bars below.

Carnelian Room. At 781 feet above the ground, enjoy dinner or cocktails here on the 52nd floor, where you may drink from the loftiest view of San Francisco's magnificent skyline. Reservations are a must for dinner here. *Top of the Bank of America Building, 555 California St., tel. 415/433-7500. Open Mon.-Thurs. 3 PM-midnight, Fri. 3 PM-1 AM, Sat. 4 PM-1 AM, Sunday 10 AM-midnight.*

Crown Room. Just ascending to the well-named Crown Room is a drama in itself as you take the Fairmont's glass-enclosed Skylift elevator to the top. Some San Franciscans maintain that this lounge is the most luxurious of the city's skyline bars. Lunches, dinners, and Sunday brunches are served as well as drinks. *29th floor of the Fairmont Hotel, California and Mason Sts., tel. 415/772-5131. Open daily 11 AM-1 AM.*

Equinox. What's distinctive about the Hyatt Regency's skyline-view bar is its capacity to revolve atop its 22nd floor perch, offering 360-degree views to guests from their seats. *At the Hyatt Regency, 5 Embarcadero Center, tel. 415/788-1234. Open Mon.-Sat. 11 AM-2:30 PM and 6 PM-1:30 AM, Sun. 11 AM-3:30 PM.*

Top of the Mark. This fabled landmark affords fabulous views in an elegant 19th-floor setting. *In the Mark Hopkins Hotel, California and Mason Sts., tel. 415/392-3434. Open nightly 4 PM-1:30 AM.*

View Lounge. Found on the 39th floor of the San Francisco Marriott, one of the newest and loveliest of the city's skyline lounges features live piano music. *777 Market St., tel. 415/896-1600. Open noon-2 AM daily.*

Singles Bars

Ever notice how everyone looks so much better when you visit another town? That same sleight of eye happens here, too. If you're young, single, and free—and like that extra edge potential romance lends to a night spot—don your best duds and head to:

Harry Denton's. The liveliest, trendiest, most upscale saloon to open in San Francisco in years, Denton's is packed with well-dressed young professionals. Its location on the Embarcadero, where the freeway recently came down, affords stunning views of the bay from the back bar. *161 Steuart St., tel. 415/882–1333. Open daily 5:30 PM–2 AM (kitchen closes at 10:30). Dancing after 10 Thurs.–Sat.*

The Holding Company. This is one of the most popular weeknight Financial District watering holes, where scores of office workers gather to enjoy friendly libations. *In 2 Embarcadero Center, tel. 415/986–0797. Open Mon.–Tues. until midnight, Wed.–Fri. until 2 AM. Closed weekends.*

Johnny Love's. The popular Mr. Love, formerly of Harry Denton's, opened his own place at the base of Russian Hill. It became an instant hit, and one of *the* places to be seen. Live music (heavy on the R&B) nightly. *1500 Broadway, at Polk St., tel. 415/931–8021. Bar is open 5 PM–2 AM nightly (dinner from 6–10). Major cards accepted.*

Perry's. Usually jam-packed, Perry's is the most famous of San Francisco's singles bars. You can dine here on great hamburgers as well as more substantial fare. *1944 Union St. at Buchanan St., tel. 415/922–9022. Open daily 9 AM–2 AM.*

San Francisco's Favorite Bars

Locals patronize all of the places listed above, but there are several joints they hold near and dear:

Buena Vista. Even though the Buena Vista's claim of having introduced Irish coffee to the New World may be dubious, this is the Wharf area's most popular bar. Usually packed with tourists, it has a fine view of the waterfront. *2765 Hyde St., near Fisherman's Wharf, tel. 415/474–5044.*

Edinburgh Castle. This is a delightful Scottish drinking emporium, with a jukebox that breathes Scottish airs and live bagpipes on weekends. The decor is Scottish, the bartender is Scottish, and there are plenty of Scottish brews from which to choose. You can work off the fish-and-chips variety fare with a turn at the dart board. *950 Geary St. near Polk St., tel. 415/885-4074.*

House of Shields. For a taste of an authentic old-time San Francisco saloon, try this bar, which attracts an older, Financial District crowd after work. It closes at 8 PM. *39 New Montgomery St., tel. 415/392-7732.*

John's Grill. Located on the fringe of the Tenderloin, this bar was featured in *The Maltese Falcon* and mystery fans will revel in its Hammett memorabilia. *63 Ellis St., tel. 415/986-0069.*

Vesuvio Cafe. Near the legendary City Lights Bookstore, this quintessentially North Beach bar is little altered since its heyday as a haven for the Beat poets. *255 Columbus Ave. between Broadway and Pacific Ave., tel. 415/362-3370.*

Gay and Lesbian Nightlife

In the days before the gay liberation movement, bars were more than mere watering holes. They also served as community centers where members of a mostly undercover minority could network and socialize. In the 1960s, they became hotbeds of political activity. The Tavern Guild of San Francisco, comprising the town's major gay establishments, achieved several of the community's first political victories, waging and winning a legal and public relations battle to end police harassment. Even teetotaling gays benefitted from the confrontation. By the 1970s, other social opportunities became available to gay men and lesbians, and the bars' importance as centers of activity decreased. Old-timers wax nostalgic about the vibrancy of pre-AIDS, '70s bar life, but plenty of fun is still to be had today. There's one difference, though: some of the best clubs operate only one night per week at a location that may have a completely different (sometimes straight) clientele on other nights. A one-nighter that has been running for a few years is Friday-only **Dekadence** at the **End Up** at Sixth and Harrison, which on other nights is a lesbian hot spot (Saturday) or home to an afternoon Tea Dance (Sunday). Anything goes at Dekadence, where punks and drag queens of all genders party down. It's a trip.

The one-night-a-week clubs tend to come and go, so it's best to pick up one of the two main gay papers: the *Bay Area Reporter* (tel. 415/861–5019 to find out where to pick up a copy) or the *San Francisco Bay Times* (tel. 415/626–8121). Both are usually available at the clubs listed below.

The papers reveal something else: there's more to gay nightlife than the bars. Most nights, **Theatre Rhinoceros** (tel. 415/861–5079) offers plays or solo shows on two stages and **Josie's Cabaret** features work by cutting-edge performance, comedy, and theater artists. Members of the Tavern Guild (tel. 415/752–2366) and Japantown Bowling (tel. 415/921–6200) leagues compete Monday–Thursday nights. City College's Gay and Lesbian Studies Department (tel. 415/239–3383) holds Monday–Thursday classes (6:30–9:30 PM) in film, literature, and other topics at Everett Middle School, 17th Street at Church (it's almost always OK to drop in for a session). Check the gay papers' extensive calendar listings for other activities.

Lesbian Bars Surprisingly, for a place known as a "gay" mecca, at present there are only two seven-day-a-week women's bars and a few reliable one-nighters (call ahead to be sure they are still operating). Younger lesbians and gays, some of whom prefer to call themselves "queers," don't segregate themselves quite as much as the older set; you'll find mixed crowds at a number of the bars listed under Gay Men's Bars, below.

The Café. Formerly Café San Marcos, this bar in the heart of the gay Castro district is always comfortable and often crowded. Chat quietly at one end or cut the rug at the other. *2367 Market St. at 17th, tel. 415/861–3846. Open noon–2 AM.*
Faster Pussycat. A fun-loving crowd engages in "shedonism in all its glory," with popular DJ Downtown Donna and others. *At Paula's Clubhouse, 3160 16th St., ½ block below Guerrero St., tel. 415/621–5877. Doors open at 8 PM, though the real fun starts after 10. Wed. nights only.*
Girlspot. The best place for a lesbian to be on Saturday night, this hot spot (aka G-Spot) features good dance music, mostly pop (Whitney Houston, etc.,) with a bit of technobeat. *At the*

End-Up, 6th and Harrison Sts., tel. 415/543-7700. Doors open at 9 PM. Sat. only.

Red Dora's Bearded Lady Café and Cabaret. This neighborhood venue serves a predominantly (though not totally) lesbian/gay clientele. It's also a gallery (mostly women's work) and music outlet for local independent labels. *485 14th St., at Guerrero St., tel. 415/626–2805. Open Sun.–Thurs. 7 AM–7 PM, Fri. and Sat. 9 AM–10:30 PM. Weekend performances (cover varies from $3–$10) begin at 8 PM. No alcohol served.*

Gay Male Bars "A bar for every taste, that's the ticket," was how the curious "documentary" *Gay San Francisco* described late-'60s nightlife here. Leather bars, drag queen hangouts, piano bars, and bohemian cafés were among the many options for gay men back then. The scene remains just as versatile today.

The SoMa Scene **The End Up.** Patrons here cruise and carouse in the open-air courtyard or work up a sweat on the spacious dance floor. The bar hosts Dekadence on Friday, Girlspot on Saturdays, and a 6 AM Tea Dance on Sunday mornings. *6th and Harrison Sts., tel. 415/543–7700. Open nightly until 2 AM, after hours (no alcohol) some weekends. Cover: none most weeknights, variable on weekends.*

Esta Noche. Latino gays, including some of the city's wildest drag queens, dance and hang out at this longtime Mission District establishment. *3079 16th St., below Valencia, tel. 415/861–5757. Open 1 PM–2 AM. Cover: weeknights none, $4 Fri.–Sun.*

SF-Eagle. In the days before AIDS and gentrification, SoMa was the headquarters for the gay leather set, with a dozen or so bars along Folsom and Harrison streets. Of the few that remain, the SF-Eagle is by far the most popular. International leather legend Mister Marcus (to you) drops by to judge the Mr. SF Leather, Mr. Leather Calendar, and innumerable other contests, most of which are AIDS benefits. *12th and Harrison Sts., tel. 415/626–0880. Open weekdays 4 PM–2 AM, weekends 2 PM–2 AM. No cover (except for special events).*

The Stud. Still going strong after 28 years, this hip club's DJs mix up-to-the-minute music with carefully chosen highlights from the glory days of gay disco. *Harrison and Ninth Sts., tel. 415/ 863–6623. Open Mon.–Sat. 5 PM–2 AM, Sun. 3 PM–2 AM.*

In the Castro **Café Flore.** Poets, punks, and poseurs mingle day and night at open-air tables or inside the glass walls of this bohemian bistro, which serves beer, wine, coffee, and tea. A separate concessionaire serves surprisingly tasty food until 9 PM, though most people come only for drinks or dessert. *2298 Market St., tel. 415/621–8579. Open daily 7:30 AM–11:30 PM.*

The Elephant Walk. One of the Castro's cozier bars, this is among the few (along with Moby Dick, at 18th and Hartford Sts., and Twin Peaks, at 17th and Castro Sts.) where the music level allows for easy conversation. *Castro St., at 18th St. no phone. Open 11 AM–2 AM.*

The Metro. Just down Market from the Detour is the more upscale Metro, whose balcony overlooks the intersection of Noe, 16th, and Market streets. "Guppies" ("gay yuppies") love this place, which has a fairly good restaurant adjoining the bar. *3600 16th St., at Market St., tel. 415/ 703–9750. Open 3:30 PM–2 AM.*

The MidnightSun. This is one of the Castro's longest-standing and most popular bars, with giant video screens riotously programmed. Don't expect to hear yourself think. *4067 18th St., tel. 415/861–4186. Open noon–2 AM.*

On/Near Polk Street **The Cinch.** Country-western music rules in this neighborhood bar, one of several in the city that hosts the gay San Francisco Pool Association's weekly matches. *1723 Polk St., tel. 415/776– 4162. Open 6 AM–2 AM.*

Kimo's. Floor-to-ceiling windows provide a great view of Polk Street action from this laid-back club. Six-foot drag queen (and former seminarian) Tatiana has raised thousands at her "First Saturday" all-star AIDS benefits. *1551 Polk St., tel. 415/885–4535. Open 9 AM–2 AM.*

Around Town **Lily's.** This bar, named in honor of one of the city's memorable drag queens, "Empress" Lily Street, is frequented by members of the city's "Imperial Court." For an intriguing earful of local gay history, ask one of the regulars how the Court system operates. *4 Valencia St., at Market St., tel. 415/864–7208. Open 11 AM–2 AM.*

Sutter's Mill. A longtime favorite with the gay Financial District set, this bar is usually packed for lunch (served 11:30–3) and right after work. *10 Mark La., off Bush St. between Grant Ave. and Kearny St., tel. 415/788–8377. Open weekdays 10:30–10.*

Index

WHEREVER YOU TRAVEL, *H*ELP IS NEVER FAR AWAY.

From planning your trip to providing travel assistance along the way, American Express® Travel Service Offices* are always there to help.

SAN FRANCISCO
237 Post St.
415-981-5533

455 Market St.
415-512-8250

295 California St.
415-788-4367

Sheraton
Fisherman's Wharf
2500 Mason St.
415-788-3025

CARMEL
Bob McGinnis Travel, Inc.
561 Carmel Rancho
Shopping Center
408-624-2724

NAPA
Thompson Travel Service
3308 Jefferson St.
707-255-8737

OAKLAND
500 12th St., Suite 115
510-834-2833

PALO ALTO
393 Stanford Shopping Center
415-327-3711

SAN RAFAEL
Terra Linda Travel
515 Northgate Dr.
415-492-0333

WALNUT CREEK
Broadway Plaza
91 Broadway Lane
510-938-0800